Wrestling

THE UNITED STATES NAVAL INSTITUTE, publisher of the Naval Aviation Physical Training Manuals, is a nation-wide organization of military and civilian members and affiliations. The Institute was founded, not for profit, but for the advancement of professional, literary, and scientific knowledge in the Navy and among military and civilian contemporaries.

THE INSTITUTE has assumed the responsibility of keeping the Naval Aviation Physical Training Manuals revised and up-to-date in every respect for use by the military services in event of national emergency. Maintenance of high standards of physical fitness in the youth of our nation is considered a prerequisite to national preparedness. With this in mind every effort has been made to insure revisions, through the V-Five Association of America, that are compatible with civilian educational interests.

# The Naval Aviation Physical Training Manuals

*Revised by the*
*V-Five Association of America*

BOARD OF DIRECTORS

OFFICERS AND BOARD MEMBERS

*Executive Chairman*
RADM. Thomas J. Hamilton, USN
(Ret)
Director of Athletics
University of Pittsburgh

*President*
Harvey J. Harman
Coach of Football
Rutgers University

*First Past-President*
Frank H. Wickhorst
Kaiser Services
Oakland, California

*First Vice-President*
Mitchell J. Gary
Director of Athletics
Western Michigan College

*Second Past-President*
W. Madison Bell
Director of Athletics
Southern Methodist University

*Second Vice-President*
Bernard W. Bierman
Coach of Football
University of Minnesota

*Board Members at Large*

CDR. William R. Kane, USN
U. S. Naval Aviation
U. S. Air Force University

Laurence A. Mullins
Director of Athletics
Saint Ambrose College

Donald B. Faurot
Director of Athletics
University of Missouri

Charles M. Speidel
Coach of Wrestling
Pennsylvania State College

Leonard J. Casanova
Coach of Football
University of Santa Clara

Charles B. Wilkinson
Coach of Football
University of Oklahoma

*Executive Director*

M. Budd Cox
V-Five Association
Annapolis, Maryland

# REVISION STAFF

**Supervising Editor**
Harold E. Lowe, Chairman
Department of Physical Education
Columbia University

**Cartoonists and Illustrators**
Ensign Elizabeth Bunker, W-VS, USNR

Martin A. Topper, District Supervisor
of Health and Physical Education
Chicago Board of Education

Robert C. Osborn
(The Dilbert Series)
Salsbury, Connecticut

## REVISION COMMITTEES

### BASKETBALL

*Co-Chairman*
Gordon H. Ridings
Coach of Basketball
Columbia University

*Co-Chairman*
LCDR. Kenneth A. Hashagen, USNR
Coach of Basketball
U. S. Naval Air Station, Memphis

*Advisory Member*
Justin M. Barry
Coach of Basketball
University of Southern California

### BOXING

*Chairman*
Roy D. Simmons
Coach of Boxing
Syracuse University

*Advisory Member*
Ike F. Deeter
Coach of Boxing
Washington State College

*Advisory Member*
LCDR. Anthony J. Rubino, USNR
Instructor in Physical Training
U. S. Naval Academy

### CONDITIONING EXERCISES, GAMES, TESTS

*Co-Chairman*
Karl C. H. Oermann, Director
of Teacher Education in Physical
Education for Men
University of Pittsburgh

*Co-Chairman*
Carl H. Young, Chairman
Department of Physical Education
University of California
Los Angeles

*Advisory Member*
Mitchell J. Gary, Director
of Athletics and Physical Education
Western Michigan College

### FOOTBALL

*Chairman*
Don B. Faurot
Coach of Football
University of Missouri

*Advisory Member*
W. Madison Bell
Coach of Football
Southern Methodist University

*Advisory Member*
Bernard W. Bierman
Coach of Football
University of Minnesota

### GYMNASTICS AND TUMBLING

*Chairman*
Hartley D. Price
Coach of Gymnastics
Florida State University

*Advisory Member*
Joseph M. Hewlett
Coach of Gymnastics
Ohio State University

*Advisory Member*
Newton C. Loken
Coach of Gymnastics
University of Michigan

## Hand-to-Hand Combat

*Chairman*
LCDR. Wesley Brown, Jr., USNR
Director of Athletics
U. S. Naval Air Station, Memphis

*Advisory Member*
Joseph W. Begala
Coach of Wrestling
Kent State University

## Intramural Programs

*Chairman*
Lloyd H. Lux, Director
of Athletics and Physical Education
Bates College

*Advisory Member*
Allen B. Klingel
Director of Recreational Sports
University of Illinois

*Advisory Member*
Charles F. Kerr
State Supervisor of Physical Education
Tennessee State Department of Education

## Soccer

*Chairman*
Earle C. Waters
Coach of Soccer
State Teachers College
West Chester, Pennsylvania

*Advisory Member*
John R. Eiler
Coach of Soccer
State Teachers College
Slippery Rock, Pennsylvania

*Advisory Member*
A. E. Florio
Assistant Professor of
Physical Education
University of Illinois

## Swimming and Diving

*Chairman*
Alfred R. Barr
Coach of Swimming
Southern Methodist University

*Advisory Member*
Ben F. Grady
Coach of Swimming
University of Pittsburgh

*Advisory Member*
LCDR. John H. Higgins, USNR
Senior Swimming Instructor
Naval School Pre-Flight
U. S. Naval Air Station, Pensacola

## Track and Field

*Co-Chairman*
Charles D. Werner
Coach of Track
Pennsylvania State College

*Co-Chairman*
Frank J. Ryan
Assistant Coach of Track
Yale University

*Advisory Member*
Laurence N. Snyder
Coach of Track
Ohio State University

## Wrestling

*Chairman*
Clifford P. Keen
Coach of Wrestling
University of Michigan

*Advisory Member*
David C. Bartelma
Coach of Wrestling
University of Minnesota

*Advisory Member*
Charles M. Speidel
Coach of Wrestling
Pennsylvania State College

# WRESTLING

*Revision Staff*

*Chairman*
Clifford P. Keen
Coach of Wrestling
University of Michigan

*Advisory Member*
David C. Bartelma
Coach of Wrestling
University of Minnesota

*Advisory Member*
Charles M. Speidel
Coach of Wrestling
Pennsylvania State College

*Supervising Editor*
Harold E. Lowe, Chairman
Department of Physical Education
Columbia University

*Executive Editor*
M. Budd Cox
V-Five Association
Annapolis, Maryland

**First Edition Staff**
(Please see Preface)

*Directors*

RADM. Thomas J. Hamilton, USN
(Ret)

CDR. Frank H. Wickhorst, USNR

*Compiler-Writer*
CDR. Clifford P. Keen, USNR

*Editorial Staff*

CDR. Harold E. Lowe, USNR

LCDR. Gordon H. Ridings, USNR

*The Naval Aviation Physical Training Manuals*

# WRESTLING

*Revised Edition*

PREPARED BY THE
V-FIVE ASSOCIATION OF AMERICA

*First Edition*

PREPARED BY OFFICERS OF THE
AVIATION TRAINING DIVISION
OFFICE OF THE CHIEF OF NAVAL OPERATIONS
UNITED STATES NAVY

*Annapolis, Maryland*

UNITED STATES NAVAL INSTITUTE

*Wrestling*
by United States Naval Institute

Copyright © 1943, 1950, 1957, 1961, 1964
by the United States Naval Institute, Annapolis, Maryland

ISBN 10: 1-58160-489-0
ISBN 13: 978-1-58160-489-4
Printed in the United States of America

Published by Paladin Press, a division of
Paladin Enterprises, Inc.
Gunbarrel Tech Center
7077 Winchester Circle
Boulder, Colorado 80301 USA
+1.303.443.7250

Direct inquiries and/or orders to the above address.

PALADIN, PALADIN PRESS, and the "horse head" design
are trademarks belonging to Paladin Enterprises and
registered in United States Patent and Trademark Office.

All rights reserved by the United States Naval Institute. Except for use in
a review, no portion of this book may be reproduced in any form without
the express written permission of the United States Naval Institute.

Neither the author nor the publisher assumes
any responsibility for the use or misuse of
information contained in this book.

Visit the United States Naval Institute Web site at www.usni.org

Visit our Web site at www.paladin-press.com

# Preface

THE Naval Aviation V-5 Physical Training Manuals were prepared and published during World War II to provide the best standardized instruction in the sports selected to give the youths, training to be combat Naval pilots, the maximum physical and psychological benefits. It was the first time that intensive athletic training was used militarily, not only for conditioning and recreation, but to develop and intensify desired qualities, such as quick reaction, coordination, accurate timing, cool judgment, aggressiveness, and determination. It was, without question, the most rigorous mass program conducted in this country utilizing a large group of different sports. Each cadet was required to spend four to six hours a day in intense athletic training for eight months, the time diminishing in later months as other elements of flight and ground training were added. The results were highly successful as proven by the testimony of the high performance of this group of pilots, and the acclaim given them and the training methods by all who observed.

Over two thousand of the nation's leading physical educators and coaches of all sports participated in the planning and operation of this program as Reserve Officers, and most of them actually contributed in the preparation of these Manuals in their own specialty. While in some instances only one author did the final writing, it may in truth be said that the project was conceived and carried out as a group enterprise. The names of those officers who originally compiled and wrote the manuals now appear with the committees of revisions opposite the title page, and we deeply regret that space does not permit acknowledgment of the contribution of literally hundreds of others whose assistance was substantial. The original edition of these manuals was completed in 1943 under the direction of Commander Frank H. Wickhorst, USNR, Head of the Naval Aviation V-5 Physical Training Program at that time.

These books have found a wide usage in the civilian field of instruction in sports and have been adapted as text books and coaching manuals throughout the country. The Navy, recognizing the valuable service the manuals perform, authorized the V-Five Association, a peace time non-profit organization, whose nucleus is the above group of officers, to revise the books. The revisions are aimed to make the volumes fully up-to-date, with added material to treat with new techniques and emphasis, and to adapt the experience and lessons learned for instruction in proper gradations at the college and high school level.

It is increasingly evident that participation in a well rounded physical training and sports program integrated with academic and spiritual elements is highly desirable in a youth's training. Different sports can be increasingly effective in developing many splendid qualities, and contribute to the well-being of the individual and the nation. It is hoped this V-5 Sports Series will continue to contribute to the general welfare of our youth.

T. J. Hamilton
Rear Admiral, USN (Ret)
Director of Athletics
University of Pittsburgh

# Introduction to First Edition

THE fundamentals of wrestling are presented in this manual for the purpose of aiding the officer in teaching wrestling to the cadets in the Naval Aviation Physical Training Program. The authors recognize that it would be inadvisable and perhaps impossible for the instructor to teach or for the cadet to learn all the holds and maneuvers contained in this book with such precision that they could be used in competition. However, every hold described has been proved and tested by champions. They are all feasible and fundamentally sound. But to make any of them work will require diligent practice and expert timing. Holds or groups of holds which will work for one wrestler will not work for another, because of physical differences and reactions. It is far better to master a few holds than to learn a little about many and master none. Four or five Take-downs, three or four Rides, four or five Pinning Combinations, and five or six Escapes should be mastered by each wrestler, and as much learned in addition as time and desire permit. There are few champions who employ more than this number of holds in actual competition. Technique and precision in the execution of holds that have been learned is by far the most important consideration. *It is more desirable to practice exhaustively on perfect timing and execution of a limited number of holds and maneuvers, with particular attention being given to the grouping of holds, than to spend the time in just getting a smattering of many.*

In the Naval Aviation Physical Training Program, it has been found that interest is enhanced in squadron competition by permitting each squadron instructor to work up his own selection of holds and maneuvers rather than to have one limited set to be used by all.

It has been our purpose to present this material simply and in a clear and understandable manner. The maneuvers are described and illustrated in their progressive stages.

This work represents the results of years of study, research and coaching experiences. It is expected that any athletic officer regardless of previous wrestling experience will be enabled to do an efficient job of coaching this sport by making a careful study and application of the fundamentals and principles outlined in this book.

# Introduction to Revised Edition

THE PURPOSE of revising this manual is to adapt the material to the needs of high school and college coaches as well as for the use of instructors of wrestling in physical training classes. The further objective is to present new trends of technique in our rapidly developing sport of wrestling and to adjust the material so as to have it conform to our present rules.

The authors recognize that it would be inadvisable and perhaps impossible for the instructor to teach, or for a team-member to learn, all the holds and maneuvers contained in this book with such precision that they could be used in competition. However, every hold described has been proved and tested by champions. They are all feasible and fundamentally sound. But to make any of them work will require diligent practice and expert timing. Holds or groups of holds which will work for one wrestler will not work for another, because of physical differences and reactions. It is far better to master a few holds than to learn a little about many and master none. Four or five Take-downs, three or four Rides, four or five Pinning Combinations, and five or six Escapes should be mastered by each wrestler, and as much learned in addition as time and desire permit. There are few champions who employ more than this number of holds in actual competition. Technique and precision in the execution of holds that have been learned is by far the most important consideration. IT IS MORE DESIRABLE TO PRACTICE EXHAUSTIVELY ON PERFECT TIMING AND EXECUTION OF A LIMITED NUMBER OF HOLDS AND MANEUVERS, WITH PARTICULAR ATTENTION BEING GIVEN TO THE GROUPING OF HOLDS, THAN TO SPEND THE TIME IN JUST GETTING A SMATTERING OF MANY.

In the Naval Aviation Physical Training Program, it has been found that interest is enhanced in squadron competition by permitting each squadron instructor to work up his own selection of holds and maneuvers rather than to have one limited set to be used by all.

It has been our purpose to present this material simply and in a clear and understandable manner. The maneuvers are described and illustrated in their progressive stages.

This work represents the results of years of study, research, and coaching experiences. It is expected that any athletic coach regardless of previous wrestling experience will be enabled to do an efficient job of coaching this sport by making a careful study and application of the fundamentals and principles outlined in this book.

THE REVISION COMMITTEE
C. P. K.
D. C. B.
C. M. S.

# Table of Contents

| | PAGE |
|---|---|
| STAFF (Revised Edition of All Manuals) | iii |
| STAFF (Revised and First Editions of Wrestling Manual) | vi |
| PREFACE | ix |
| INTRODUCTION (First Edition) | xi |
| INTRODUCTION (Revised Edition) | xii |

CHAPTER
- I  A Brief History of Wrestling .................................................. 3
- II  Value of Wrestling in an Athletic Program .................................... 7
- III  Facilities, Gear, and Safety Devices ......................................... 10
    - Facilities .................................................................. 10
    - Gear ....................................................................... 11
    - Safety Devices ............................................................. 11
- IV  Care and Prevention of Injuries .............................................. 13
    - Cauliflower Ears ........................................................... 13
    - Impetigo and Boils ......................................................... 14
    - Sprains, Dislocations, and Broken Bones .................................... 14
    - General .................................................................... 14
- V  Developing a Team for Competition ............................................. 15
    - Strategy ................................................................... 16
    - Chain Wrestling ............................................................ 17
    - Conditioning a Varsity Team ................................................ 17
    - Developing a Varsity Team .................................................. 19
        - Weight Control ......................................................... 20
        - Diet, Sleep, and Training .............................................. 21
        - "Staleness" ............................................................ 21
    - Development of a Physical Training Class or Squadron Team .................. 21
- VI  Take Downs and Counters ...................................................... 22
    - Stance ..................................................................... 22
    - Setting Up a Single or Double Leg Tackle ................................... 23
    - The Single Leg Tackle ...................................................... 25
    - The Double Leg Tackle ...................................................... 29
    - Double Leg Pick Up and Back Heel ........................................... 30
    - The Double Leg Tackle, Pick Up, Crotch, and Half Nelson .................... 31
    - Counters for Leg Tackles and Leg Pick Ups .................................. 32
    - Crotch Lift and Back Heel .................................................. 35
    - Crotch Lift and Half Nelson ................................................ 35
    - Counters for a Crotch Lift ................................................. 36
    - Head Under Arm and Back Heel ............................................... 37
    - Head Under Arm Sneak ....................................................... 37
    - Head Under Arm Series ...................................................... 38
        - Head Under Arm and Crotch Lift ......................................... 38

Head Under Arm and Arm Pull .................................................. 39
The Double Arm Lock and Roll ................................................. 39
Counters for Head Under Arm Situations ...................................... 40
The Head Under Arm Spin ........................................................ 40
The Merry Go Round ............................................................... 41
The Double Arm Lock .............................................................. 42
Counter for a Double Arm Lock .................................................. 42
Head Chancery and Bar Arm ..................................................... 42
Counter for Head Chancery and Bar Arm ..................................... 43
Double Bar Arm Lock ............................................................... 43
Block for Double Bar Arm Lock .................................................. 43
Counter for Double Bar Arm Lock ............................................... 43
Whizzer Series ........................................................................ 44
Counters for Whizzer Holds ....................................................... 47
Head and Far Heel Pick Up ....................................................... 47
Head and Near Heel Pick Up ..................................................... 48
Block for Head and Heel Pick Up ............................................... 48
Single Arm Drag ..................................................................... 48
Counters for Single Arm Drag .................................................... 52
Double Wrist Lock ................................................................... 53
Block for a Double Wrist Lock .................................................... 53
Counter for a Double Wrist Lock ................................................. 53
Side Head Lock ...................................................................... 54
Counters for Side Headlock ....................................................... 55

VII  GO BEHIND FROM HEAD ON .................................................... 56
Head On Position .................................................................... 57
Go Behinds from Top Side ......................................................... 57
Go Behinds from Down Under .................................................... 58

VIII TAKING TO MAT FROM STANDING ............................................. 59
Standing Rear Body Lock .......................................................... 59

IX   ESCAPES FROM STANDING ....................................................... 63
Standing Rear Body Lock .......................................................... 63

X    BREAKDOWNS AND RIDES ........................................................ 66
Riding .................................................................................. 66
  Point of Contact Drill ............................................................. 67
  Break Downs ....................................................................... 67
  Body Scissors ..................................................................... 72

XI   PINNING COMBINATIONS ......................................................... 76
Inside Crotch Pinning Combinations ............................................ 76
  Bar Lock and Half Nelson ....................................................... 77
  Bar Lock and Figure Four Head Scissors .................................... 78
  Bar Lock and Farther Under Arm Hook ....................................... 79
  Arm Lock and Body Press ...................................................... 82
  Modified Three Quarter Nelson ................................................ 82
  Double Bar Arm Lock ............................................................ 83
  Chicken Wing (The Bar Hammerlock) ........................................ 84
  Body Scissors ..................................................................... 85
  Counters for Pin Holds .......................................................... 89

# TABLE OF CONTENTS

| | | |
|---|---|---|
| XII | Escapes from Underneath | 92 |
| | Stance | 92 |
| | The Tripod Position | 92 |
| | Switch | 97 |
| | The Double Wrist Lock | 99 |
| | The Sit Out | 101 |
| | The Forward Roll | 103 |
| | The Power Craw Fish | 104 |
| | Elevators | 104 |
| | The Step Over | 108 |
| | Slipping a Near Half Nelson | 108 |
| XIII | Escapes from Special Rides | 109 |
| | Escapes from Cross Body Ride | 109 |
| | Escape from Crab Ride | 111 |
| | Escape from Stretcher | 111 |
| | Escape from Figure Four Scissors | 112 |
| | Escapes from Ankle Ride | 112 |
| | Escape from Over Leg Ride | 113 |
| XIV | Counters for Common Methods of Escape | 114 |
| | Counters for the Stand Up | 114 |
| | Counters for the Sit Out | 115 |
| | Counter for Power Craw Fish | 116 |
| | Counters for the Switch | 117 |
| | Counters for Double Wrist Lock | 118 |
| | Counter for the Side Roll | 119 |
| | Counter for the Elevator | 120 |
| XV | Method for Giving Class Instruction | 121 |
| | Raised Instruction Platform | 121 |
| | The Whistle | 121 |
| | The Warm Up | 123 |
| | Modified Combat Games | 123 |
| | "No Fall" Wrestling | 128 |
| | Instructions for the Conduct of Tournaments | 129 |
| |     Tournament Forms and Score Sheets | 130 |
| |     Dual Meet Score Sheet | 135 |
| | Suggestions to Referees | 136 |
| XVI | The Olympic Style of Wrestling | 138 |
| | Standing Tactics | 140 |
| | Escapes | 144 |
| | Pinning Combinations | 147 |
| | United States Olympic Wrestling Team (1948) | 154 |
| | Appendix—The Naval Aviation Wrestling Program | 155 |
| | Class Organization | 157 |
| |     Military | 157 |
| |     Informal | 157 |
| | Specific Examples of Giving Class Instruction in Drill Form | 158 |
| |     The Single Arm Drag | 158 |
| |     The Side Roll | 158 |

       The Crotch Pry Break Down—Completed with a Near Bar Lock Ride ...... 158
       The Bar Lock and Half Nelson ................................... 159
       Give Them Plenty of Work ...................................... 159
       Creating and Maintaining Interest ................................ 159
    Lesson Plans ..................................................... 161
INDEX ................................................................ 179

# WRESTLING

## The Battle of Life

By
Theodore Roosevelt

"In the battle of life it is not the critic who counts; not the man who points out how the strong man stumbled, or where the doer of a deed could have done better. The credit belongs to the man who is actually in the arena; whose face is marred by dust and sweat and blood; who strives valiantly; who errs and comes short again and again because there is no effort without error and shortcoming; who does actually strive to do the deeds; who knows the great enthusiasms, the great devotion, spends himself in a worthy cause; who at the best knows in the end the triumph of high achievement; and who at the worst, if he fails, at least fails while daring greatly, so that his place shall never be with those cold and timid souls who have tasted neither victory nor defeat.

"He who will make a wise use of any part of his life must allot a goodly portion of it to recreation."

# CHAPTER I
# A Brief History of Wrestling

Wrestling is one of the oldest forms of combat of which we have any record. Even before the historic era, we are reasonably sure that the Stone Age man developed a form of wrestling which bordered on the scientific. Stone Age man had to provide for himself by means of strength and cunning: consequently, physical combat was essential. Wrestling at that time was not only the primary type of warfare between men but also extended to the conflicts between men and beasts. Consequently, in this Age wrestling was of a significantly brutal form.

At the dawn of civilization, wrestling was an art of war. Though still of a savage nature among the Egyptians and Assyrians (3000 B.C.), it was yet a manly art. The scenes sculptured upon the walls of the temple-tombs of Beni Hasan near the Nile show a multitude of wrestling matches depicting practically all the holds and fall combinations known at the present time. Thus, we know for a certainty that wrestling was a highly developed combative sport even at that early date.

Since warfare at this early date was necessarily based on close contact struggle, it awarded victory to the strongest a nd most virile race and not to the possessor of the most diabolical engines of war. This kind of warfare had the advantage of emphasizing manhood and personal bravery as opposed to the use of cold-blooded cunning and trickery which masquerades at present under the euphonious title of strategy.

Many references are made to wrestling matches in the Bible. It was an ancient method used in settling disputes and because of this practice some knowledge of wrestling had to be possessed by any man who wished to retain his self-respect among his fellows. Hence, wrestling progressed through the ages until it became a sport in the modern sense of the word.

This sport, in a systematic and scientific form, was probably introduced into Greece from Egypt or Asia. Though Greek tradition ascribed its invention and original rules to the legendary hero, Theseus, Homer's description of holds corresponds closely with the Beni Hasan figures. Wrestling was a very important branch of athletics in the Greek games and it was the heart of Greek sports since it formed the chief event of the Pentathlon, or Quintruple games. From writings of great historians, it is evident that wrestling was the favorite exercise in Greek athletic training. It was from wrestling that the Palaestra took its name, and the Greek language is full of metaphors and expressions which were borrowed from the technical phraseology of the wrestling ring. Women were allowed to compete in some states, even against men. Instruction was given in school; textbooks were used; in fact, fragments of such a manual have recently been found on an

Egyptian papyrus scroll. There were many types of wrestling existing in Greece in the various districts. These diversities of method maintained interest and the popularity of wrestling as a sport. It is of interest to note that Pindar and other Greek poets attribute the first Olympic festival, held beside the river Alpheus at Olympia in 776 B.C., to the result of a wrestling match between Zeus and Kronos. They tell us that these mightiest of the Gods wrestled for the possession of the earth on the high peaks above and that the games and religious celebrations held later in the valley below were in commemoration of the victory of Zeus. Later, when an athlete triumphed in the stadium, he gave public thanks to Zeus. However, wrestling as a major sport was not introduced into the Olympics until 704 B.C., at which time the 18th Olympiad was held. Another proof of the popularity of the sport in Greece is the fact that the favorite subjects for Grecian vases are struggles between their various idols, and a pose from a wrestling bout was used on one of their coins.

The Pankration, a composite of boxing and wrestling, came into practice in Greek sports. This turned out to be quite brutal.

Wrestling was introduced into Rome in the last quarter of the Second Century B.C., but it never attained Grecian popularity. To the Teutonic peoples, wrestling as a form of athletic recreation as well as a method of fighting was always practiced. The popularity it had achieved as a sport during the Middle Ages is proved by the many references to the historic personages noted for their skill in the art, and still more so by the volumes of literature on the subject which appeared after the invention of printing.

In Great Britain wrestling was developed in an early era. It is really a continuation of the history of wrestling, which was practiced centuries before by the Greeks and Romans. English literature is full of references to the sport in which the men of Cornwall held it in high esteem. The Celts and Saxons were also devoted to wrestling. Special matches took place throughout England on St. James and St. Bartholomew's days. The Lord Mayor and his sheriffs were usually present on these occasions, and all English monarchs have patronized the sport. In fact, the most famous bout between France and England is undoubtedly that of Henry the Eighth and Francis the First at the meeting of the Cloth of Gold, in 1520. The accounts of this royal encounter differ widely, but the fact that persons of so exalted a rank engaged in such a contest is the highest honor that can be given to wrestling in the Sixteenth Century. At that time the English and French kings were the foremost monarchs in Europe.

Of the Asiatic countries, perhaps China was the first in which wrestling was introduced; however, it was more popular in Japan where the first match recorded took place in the year of 22 B.C. Emperor Shomu in the Fifth Century made wrestling one of the features of the annual "Festival of the Five Grains," and Emperor Ninmyo in the Ninth Century proclaimed, "The Wrestling Festival is not only an occasion for mere amusement, but the most appropriate observance of the development of the military strength of the nation."

Although wrestling is one of our oldest sports, it did not come into prominence as an amateur sport in the United States until the last twenty years. The first organized intercollegiate wrestling meet was held between the Universities of Pennsylvania and Yale in 1900. The popularity of the sport immediately spread, and in 1904 a group of Eastern universities formed the Eastern Intercollegiate Wrestling Conference, for the purpose of drawing up a uniform set of rules to govern competition in wrestling. The first wrestling tournament was held by them in the Spring of 1905. They have continued to hold annual tournaments since and to be a very active and important organization in the development of the sport throughout the entire nation. Perhaps the greatest single influence toward the development of amateur wrestling sprang from the organization of the Wrestling Rules Committee by the National Collegiate Athletic Association in 1927. The sport was indeed fortunate to have Dr. R. G. Clapp, head of the Physical Education Department, University of Nebraska, as the chairman of the committee for many years. The background and insight of Dr. Clapp and other distinguished members of these committees have definitely aided in the development of wrestling. Prior to this time there was no uniformity of rules. It was necessary for coaches to attempt to agree on the rules, weights, length of bouts, etc., prior to engaging in any meet or tournament. Today, there is only one set of rules in effect throughout the entire nation. In addition to uniformity, there has been a constant improvement of the wrestling code. Many changes have been made which safeguard against injury and which make it the great sport it is now, both in point of interest to the contestants and to spectators. Two of the greatest improvements adopted by the National Rules Committee were: (1) a "point" system for scoring a match when no fall was secured, and (2) dividing the matches into three periods of three minutes each. Prior to the advent of the point system, the emphasis was placed on the ability of the contestant to "ride" in a position of advantage longer than his opponent. This sometimes resulted in dull and uninteresting matches with no great effort being made to secure a fall. Now, with a more complete evaluation being given for successful execution of a varied attack, the matches are filled with action, and spectator interest has been greatly increased. The matches have become spirited contests with much greater possibility for skill and versatility to be employed by the contestants.

    Today wrestling is an international sport. All countries wrestle under the same rules in the Olympic games, but aside from the style used in these games, almost every country has its own native style. There are two types of wrestling which are sponsored in the Olympic games: Graeco-Roman and Catch-as-Catch-Can. Separate competition is held in each of these two styles with different rules being followed for each style. Graeco-Roman is used extensively in Europe. In this style of wrestling, all tripping and application of holds on the legs is prohibited. A fall is obtained when one of the contestants throws his opponent to the mat so the points on each shoulder touch the mat simultaneously. In the Catch-as-Catch-Can contest, sometimes called "Free Style," wrestlers are permitted to take holds below the waist; tripping and tackling being common maneuvers. When both shoulders touch the mat simultaneously a man is also considered defeated.

    It is significant that, under Catch-as-Catch-Can rules in the Olympics over a long span of years, the United States of America has proved superiority by winning twenty-one out of a possible fifty-two championships in the various weight classes. Next in championships won is Finland with eight; Sweden six; and England three. Several nations have never won a championship in any type of Olympic wrestling competition. Turkey dominated the XIV Olympiad which was held in London in 1948 by winning four individual championships. Finland and Hungary won a single championship each.

European wrestling differs from American wrestling in that it emphasizes the ability to obtain a lock on an opponent while in a standing position and throw him to the mat for an immediate fall.

On the other hand, the American style places greater emphasis on the ability to control an opponent after he has been brought to the mat. From this position on the mat, the contestant in control attempts to work his opponent into position for a fall. In our wrestling it is necessary to hold your opponent's shoulders to the mat for a period of two seconds in order to secure a fall. We would be remiss in our duty if we failed to point out the difference in our amateur style of wrestling and that practiced by the professional wrestlers. In short, there is no similarity at all except in the name. Amateur wrestling is a sport of the highest order, with the greatest emphasis being placed on clean living, superb physical condition, competitive ability, self-mastery, and the development of the many fine techniques which are required to become proficient in real wrestling. Professional wrestling has degenerated into a hippodrome affair, where sham opponents go through all kinds of horrendous make-believe for the entertainment of the gullible public and of course for the enhancement of the box-office.

In concluding any historical sketch of the sport of wrestling, attention must be called to the fact that wrestling has developed as a sport in every civilized country in the world. It is also significant and interesting to note that the peak of civilization and the highest degree of national virility is and has been reached in every country at a time which corresponds to the greatest development of wrestling in those respective countries.

CHAPTER II

# Value of Wrestling in an Athletic Program

Wrestling is an ideal sport to prepare men for combat duty. Owing to its rigorous nature, it not only provides a fine mental tonic toward development of an aggressive attitude, but it is unexcelled as a means of acquiring physical efficiency, coordination, poise, and effective use of the body. After a man has learned how to pin his opponent's shoulders to the mat, the winning spirit invades the mind and he realizes that he "can take care of himself" in any sort of physical encounter.

All normal young men have a desire to place themselves in situations where they are on their own responsibility; with success or failure depending upon their own intelligence, skill, speed, and strength. This spirit of conquest, this desire for physical adventure, is a normal heritage of youth.

Wrestling is popular with the cadets. Every growing American boy takes pride in his physical prowess, and it is rare to find any young man who is not anxious to do everything possible toward acquiring the skill and development of his inherent physical attributes to the greatest degree possible. The desire for physical superiority extends to the entire animal kingdom. This desire is real and deep-seated, as it should be, not only for the practical value it has, but also for the tremendous psychological impetus in acquiring mental preparation for combat duty.

Competitive ability, which is one of the most noble and admirable qualities possessed or developed by man, is one of the essential ingredients for success in wrestling. All athletic coaches recognize this intangible and highly important factor and strive to bring it to a peak among the individual members composing their teams. A high premium is placed on competitive ability in wrestling. This quality is germane and essential to success in this great sport, and can be developed in wrestling to a high degree.

Boundless emphasis can be placed on competitive ability, strong moral fiber, and courage; which are indispensable to these cadets when they are called on for their big undertakings.

Awkwardness can be overcome by first learning the exact technique of important maneuvers when followed by diligent practice. Similarly, qualities which we ordinarily associate with the individual's personality, if deficient, can be developed by supplying the stimulating situation, suggesting the proper response, if necessary, and then encouraging the pupil to overcome the weakness through repeated effort in similar circumstances.

It is most regrettable that the physical training of the majority of our young men has been neglected prior to their coming into The Naval Aviation Program. If it were not for this unfortunate situation the high pressure remedial procedure to which we must resort in our Naval Aviation Physical Training Program would be unnecessary. The ideal time to teach young men the art of wrestling and other sports is in high school or junior high school during the great formative period of their lives.

In wrestling, individual sport is at its best. The wrestler is given an opportunity for self-expression which may be denied to him in team games. The wrestler need not submerge his personality and merely be a part of a machine which is directed by someone else. Once he enters the contest, the final outcome is his own responsibility. The coach cannot send in remedial advice at a crucial moment, and no substitute will appear when a wrestler's powers begin to wane. He cannot take "time out" to discuss his difficulties; he is fighting on his own responsibility and must make his own decisions; his success depends upon his own intelligence, determination, and physical powers. It is difficult to conceive of a better method of making preparation for a situation which will call for self-reliance, initiative, and ability to decide upon a course of action when pressed for time and often when in a condition of acute physical discomfort.

As wrestling is organized, it provides an outlet for the athletic ambitions of boys of all sizes and weights. The competitive matches are divided into weight classifications which permit each individual to compete against an opponent of corresponding weight. Another fine thing about wrestling is that the nature of the sport lends itself to the development of a proficiency regardless of the build of the individual. There have been champions in the 115 pound class who were over six feet in height, and heavyweight champions who were less than five feet and six inches in height. Wrestlers with peculiar builds can make adaptations to take advantage of it. To illustrate, those of the "short" variety may take advantage of their stature by developing effective Stand Ups, or Head Underarm tactics; while those on the "long" side may take advantage of their legs in application of Body Scissors holds and in having a wider base from which to control their opponent with greater mechanical leverage.

Wrestling has the practical advantage of being a most effective means of incapacitating an adversary in a rough and tumble fight without weapons. The very excellent course in Hand-to-Hand Combat which is given in the Naval Aviation Physical Training Program is predicated on and carefully co-ordinated with the course in wrestling. As a matter of fact, Hand-to-Hand Combat is nothing more than an adaptation of wrestling, boxing, jiu jitsu, and other combat sports. Tactics employed in bar-rooms and back-alley fighting are put on a scientific basis through the use of wrestling principles for obtaining the greatest mechanical advantage.

The Naval Aviation Physical Training Program is particularly designed for men who are preparing for combat. Special emphasis, therefore, is given to methods of gaining and maintaining control of an opponent so that he can be over-powered or incapacitated by the further application of Hand-to-Hand Combat tactics. A more liberal interpretation of wrestling rules is followed so the cadet may become accustomed to defending himself against foul tactics.

Wrestling is not being taught to the cadets for wrestling's sake; the niceties of the rules are not adhered to, but much concern is given to methods of man-handling an enemy.

Self-confidence is built up through the channel of frequent competition. Frequent competition tends to eliminate certain emotional restraints, develops a feeling of self-confidence, and breaks down fear of engaging in a contest which is so similar to an actual fight. We hope this sense of security will carry over into actual flying.

Wrestling helps to develop four things that a combat pilot must have:

1. *Individual initiative.*
2. *Mental alertness and physical toughness.*
3. *Body control under combat conditions.*
4. *Courage and physical efficiency to carry on.*

CHAPTER III

# Facilities, Gear and Safety Devices

Wrestling can be taught to a certain extent without facilities, if necessary. Men wrestled for years on the bare ground with no protection. The first great wrestling contests of which we have records were staged in an open arena in a circle marked off on the ground. In the Scandinavian countries, where wrestling has made a tremendous scientific development and is intensely popular with spectators, much of their wrestling is still done on the bare ground. In the United States, where we have become accustomed to finer athletic facilities and where gymnasiums are plentiful, we have confined our wrestling mostly to an inside area, and wrestle on mats made of various kinds of materials.

*Facilities*

Any large, well ventilated room that can be kept clean and in a sanitary condition is satisfactory. A space of approximately fifty square feet per individual participant should be provided. Thus, an area of 60 feet by 60 feet could conveniently accommodate 72 participants. It is desirable to have adequate space in order to decrease the possibility of injuries caused by the men falling onto each other. It is much better to divide the class or team into sections than to load the mat too heavily.

Any soft and resilient material can be used for mats, ranging from the number one hair-felt mats, preferably three inches thick, to a boxed-in saw-dust pit with a canvas cover stretched over it. If a saw-dust pit is used, there should be six inches to eight inches of saw-dust placed on the floor or ground and boxed in by using boards around the side. A canvas should be pulled tightly over the area and made secure by tacking to the side boards. Straw, excelsior, corn husks, and many other materials can be used as a filler instead of saw-dust. Where funds are not available for buying a canvas cover, it may be possible to find an old tent or use some other strong and heavy material that may be available for a covering.

There must be another covering made of a smoother material stretched over the canvas covering and secured to the side boards. It is unwise to wrestle on canvas because it is so coarse that it would cause mat burns. The best mat coverings are plastic, moleskin, or heavy canton-flannel materials.

If a soft grassy spot is available, restricted wrestling can be engaged in quite satisfactorily by stretching a cover out on the bare ground. The cover should be stretched tightly and pegged down around the edges.

It must be understood that there is more danger and greater possibility of injuries occurring when any sort of make-shift facilities are used. For that reason all the more caution should be exercised when first-class facilities are not available.

Cotton mattress type mats, preferably not less than three inches in thickness, are satisfactory. However, the most common method used where a regular wrestling mat cannot be found, is to lay gymnasium mats alongside each other. These small mats should be covered with a mat cover made from plastic, moleskin, or heavy canton-flannel material. This covering should be pulled tightly over the mats and either tucked under the outside area or preferably, held tight by means of grommets in the outer edge of the mat cover, at intervals of eight inches, and made secure to the mats by means of hooks sewed on the under side of the outer edge of the mats, or to corresponding eye-screws inserted into the floor six inches inside the outer edge of the mats. A cord interlaced between grommets and eye-screws will hold the covers tight and secure. This covering will serve the two-fold purpose of keeping the gymnasium mats from spreading and providing a soft covering to wrestle on. It is unwise to wrestle on the bare canvas mats, because the surface is so coarse that it will cause mat burns, and it is too difficult to keep the mats clean.

It is not advisable to have a single cloth mat cover larger than 30 feet square on account of the difficulty of laundering it. If a single mat area is larger than this, separate covers will have to be fastened together by means of a cord interlaced between grommets inserted along the outer edges of the mat covers.

Plastic mat covers can be used instead of cloth covers. The original cost is quite high, but they will last for years and are perhaps cheaper in the long run. Plastic covers do have the important advantage of convenience and cleanliness. They can be washed with a mild antiseptic solution contained in a bucket of water after each day's practice. A zinc stearate or other antiseptic powder can be sprinkled over the mat to overcome mat friction and to provide a sterilizing agent.

Where moleskin or canton-flannel covers are used, they should be washed frequently and sprayed with a mild antiseptic solution every day. It is also desirable to sweep them once per day with a vacuum cleaner. It is imperative that strict sanitary conditions be observed.

### *Gear*

*For Practice.*—A regular gym outfit provides adequate personal equipment. Soft rubber-soled shoes and a pair of wrestling trunks or gym pants are all that is essential. However, it is desirable to have each participant outfitted with a warm sweat-suit. They should be worn when not actually engaged in wrestling to prevent cooling off too rapidly.

*For Meet Competition.*—The uniform should consist of full length tights, close-fitting outside short trunks, light heelless gymnasium shoes laced by means of eyelets, and shirts with attached supporters. It is desirable to have all members of the team dressed neatly and in color combinations of the organization represented. Uniform bathrobes or woolen sweat-suits should be provided for each member of the team.

### *Safety Devices*

The practice area should be carefully safeguarded against all possible hazards. All joists, radiators, or projections in proximity to the wrestling area should be padded and, where the mat area is next to a wall, wall mats at least five feet high should be installed in order to prevent injury which may be caused by bumping into such hard surfaces. Supplementary mats, five feet in width, should extend entirely around the mat proper.

It is important that the mat covers be kept tight. It is an easy matter to twist an ankle or break a leg by getting a foot caught in a loose cover. Where gymnasium mats are used, care should be exercised to see that they are always pulled tightly together.

CHAPTER IV

# Care and Prevention of Injuries

The greatest single factor in preventing injuries in wrestling is good physical condition. No strenuous competition should be engaged in until some semblance of wrestling condition has been attained in accordance with methods suggested in Chapter V. An important corollary to this first principle is to warm up by the use of exercises, rope-skipping, and wrestling drills against passive resistance, before engaging in actual wrestling bouts. More strained muscles occur from attempting to wrestle when not properly warmed up than any other cause.

*Cauliflower Ears*

This condition is caused by any hard blow, rubbing, or rolling which separates the skin from the cartilage of the ear. This separation causes an inside bleeding between the cartilage and skin. If not promptly and properly treated, the blood will clot and finally change into solid tissue. This may cause the ear to become warped and wrinkled to resemble a cauliflower.

This condition can be entirely prevented by providing every member of the squad with a wrestling helmet. There are several designs of helmets which can be used to protect the ears from becoming bruised. The greatest difficulty in using helmets lies in getting the men to wear them. Many of the men are willing to take a chance on not getting their ears injured and, until recently, there were no wrestling helmets on the market which could be fitted securely enough to the head to prevent slipping and interfering when wrestling. There are at least two excellently designed helmets on the market now which give good protection. They are attached over the head and under the chin in such a manner as to interfere very little in wrestling. As a matter of fact, an ear that has been previously injured can be fairly well protected against further injury by wearing one of these properly designed helmets, inasmuch as a plastic or fabricated cup is held securely over the ears and thus prevents the injured ear from coming in contact with anything.

If the ear is injured the treatment consists of two parts. First, careful precaution must be taken against re-injury. Second, the ear must be treated by drawing the blood out from under the skin by the use of a hypodermic needle. Several aspirations may be required before the hemorrhage is finally checked and the normal thickness and contour of the ear restored. This must be done by a doctor, as there is danger of infection if the needle is not properly sterilized. After the swelling has been relieved by removal of the blood, a pressure bandage should be put on the ear to keep the skin of the ear pressed tightly to the cartilage. The best method now known of applying such pressure is to fill the auricle of the ear with built-up layers of collodion and cotton.

### Impetigo and Boils

Absolute cleanliness will prevent the contagion of either of these infections. Any member of a squad who is afflicted with either should not be permitted to continue with wrestling until he is authorized to do so by the medical authorities. And certainly the most rudimentary precepts of sportsmanship would be violated by permitting a member of a team so afflicted to compete in outside competition.

If the wrestling area has once been exposed, the mat cover should be washed and the mats sprayed with a strong antiseptic. The wrestling gear of the member, or members, afflicted or exposed should be taken up and washed in a strong antiseptic solution.

### Sprains, Dislocations and Broken Bones

Good training facilities and competent medical aid are great blessings to any athletic coach. Even though serious injuries are rare when careful supervision is given, such things may happen in any vigorous contact activity, and must be anticipated. For any serious sprain, dislocation, or broken bone, a doctor should be called immediately. Don't experiment with elementary First Aid or other remedial ideas of your own when medical attention is available. Serious injury may be caused by unnecessarily moving an injured man, trying to reduce what you believe to be a dislocated joint, or otherwise attempting to administer aid when there is a question concerning the nature of the injury.

### General

A minor ailment should not prevent working out in some manner or other. After the nature of an ailment has been determined, and it has been ascertained that no serious consequence will result from engaging in some limited activity, everything possible should be done within those limitations and without too much self-pity or regard for some slight discomfort. Wrestling is a tough sport and was not designed for weaklings. Self-discipline must be exercised; since it must be recognized that it is not easy to win in a wrestling match against a worthy opponent. Men participating in this sport should not be coddled or "babied" when suffering from minor or inconsequential injuries; but, on the other hand, there should be no neglect of proper care and medical attention to even the slightest scratch or abrasion that may develop into something more serious. Have all scratches, cuts, or mat-burns treated immediately and see that they are properly covered and taken care of until they are completely well. Men suffering from chronic injuries, such as recurring dislocations of the shoulder or loose cartilages of the knee joint, should either be prohibited from wrestling or be given restricted work that they can do safely.

CHAPTER V

# Developing a Team for Competition

Organization can, and usually does, mean the difference between a successful and a mediocre team.

In the development of a varsity team, where there is plenty of time before the wrestling season starts, a more casual procedure can be followed than in the development of an intramural, physical training, or squadron team for the Sports Program. It is desirable to have a long conditioning program before meet competition starts. A general plan should be carefully worked out, with progressive weekly schedules drawn up and with definite objectives to be accomplished for each succeeding week. A daily lesson plan should be prepared and followed as carefully as possible. The instructor must be aware of the progress his team is making, what the deficiencies are, and revise his schedule from time to time as it is deemed advisable.

A great responsibility rests upon the instructor. It is well for him to remember that he exerts a profound influence upon a group of highly impressionable young men, and at a very formative period of their lives. Wrestling has much to offer. It is up to him to see that full value is obtained. He should be dynamic, enthusiastic, fair, honorable, and at all times an inspiration to his men. His personality and attitude are injected into his team. It is a great opportunity to influence and mold the lives of proteges. Every coach should recognize that merely giving technical instruction in the science of wrestling is not the extent of his duties.

For teaching convenience, wrestling instruction should be divided into at least eight classifications:

1. Take Downs
2. Go Behinds from "Head-On"
3. Taking to Mat from Standing
4. Escapes from Standing
5. Riding and Break Downs
6. Pinning Combinations
7. Escaping from Underneath
8. Counters or Blocks for All Common Holds

Proficiency in all these departments is necessary to become expert in wrestling. No one hold, lock, counter, or maneuver is complete in itself, but is valuable only in that to which it leads. There has never been a hold devised that could not be blocked or countered by an opponent of equal ability. It is important to bear this in mind, otherwise you may come to the fallacious conclusion that there are no workable holds. Every move, push, pull, fake, or feint should be done for the purpose of setting your opponent up for the hold which is ultimately applied.

When your opponent blocks one move, he has weakened his position for an attack from another angle. It will be noted that the holds presented in the succeeding chapters are grouped in such a manner as to show the possibilities existing from a certain position or situation. All of the holds herein described should be viewed as related principles and not as a series of isolated holds or grips.

Daily lesson plans should be carefully prepared. Explanations and demonstrations should be presented in the clearest, shortest, and most forceful manner. The coach must be cognizant of the progress being made and must know exactly what material has been given on the preceding day.

Refrain from haranguing and unnecessary shouting when working with men whose powers of reception are slow. Infinite patience is required. *Always try to build the men up and never tear them down.* Encouragement and praise should be given when merited, but strict and severe disciplinary action should be enforced for infraction of rules or for a continued poor attitude. "One rotten apple should not be allowed to spoil the good ones." Wrestling is a wonderful sport; if it does not succeed, it must be the fault of the coach.

It is our purpose to present this material in a simple, concise, clear, and understandable manner. The maneuvers are described and illustrated in their progressive stages.

## STRATEGY

The members of a wrestling team should be given opportunities and suggestions from the coach to practice strategy in regular match competition. Strategy, or judgment, is the determining factor in all close matches.

The men should know and understand all the rules. They must learn to keep in mind what has transpired during the course of the match; remember what holds or maneuvers have worked; make every move count for some purpose and attempt to execute holds at the most opportune time after they have been set up. It may be advisable for the coach to stop a practice match and make corrections or suggestions as to holds that are being overlooked or as to mistakes being made.

The coach should aid his men in making the proper mental preparation for a hard match or tournament. It is desirable to know as much as possible about the tactics, points of weakness and strength, particular holds used, peculiarities, etc., of each member of the opposing team. A plan of attack should be suggested and carefully worked out with each individual member. It is desirable for the men to have a wholesome respect for the ability and prowess of their opponents, but it is equally important that they have confidence in their own ability. The coach should radiate confidence and cheerfulness and try to keep his men from worrying too much immediately preceding the match. An individual with a nervous temperament should be "toned down" by means of various subtle tactics, to obviate the possibility of his "sapping" himself through expenditure of nervous energy before the match takes place. In some cases, there may be certain "cocky" individuals on the team who may need to be cautioned against over-confidence. This condition may cause carelessness and lack of respect for an opponent and perhaps result in the use of holds that have not been properly set up. When this situation occurs, it may tend to confuse and permit losing the match to an inferior man. Or there may be certain lethargic or unemotional individuals on the team who need some "prodding" before they will make the preparation or rise to the heights necessary for them to make their best efforts.

The men should learn the importance of making their opponents carry their weight. When in a locked position they must learn how to maneuver their opponent's head under their own arm or chest. They must learn to recognize that the man in the top or over position has more possibilities of maneuvering to secure a Go Behind, in addition to making the underneath man carry the weight of both. When in the Riding position, the top man should learn how to wear his opponent down by keeping his weight properly distributed and keeping the under man knocked off balance so that he will be at the greatest disadvantage for supporting the top man's weight.

## CHAIN WRESTLING

Efficient teaching requires that different variations of a particular hold or situation be considered and taught together. This is sometimes known as "chain wrestling." That is, considering the hold or variation of any particular hold that would be the most appropriate in the light of the movement your opponent has made. The variations shown of the Single Leg Tackle is an example of what is meant by "chain wrestling." It is based on the idea of selecting your hold in accordance with the movement made by your opponent after you have initiated a particular hold or maneuver. Much practice is required to enable a wrestler to recognize or anticipate the situation instantly when an opponent has been made vulnerable for a particular hold or a variation of a particular hold.

## CONDITIONING A VARSITY TEAM

Getting a team in first-class physical condition is a matter of such prime necessity that it must require the most careful planning and an observance of the most rigid training schedule. *Superb physical condition is absolutely essential for success in wrestling.*

To begin with, all candidates for the team should be assembled and a general outline of the program submitted to them. The importance of acquiring the best physical condition possible should be emphasized. A carefully prepared training schedule should be worked out and all members of the squad be made to understand what is expected of them. All regulations and rules of conduct that are to be maintained during the course of the season should be announced. At this time all the men should be informed that wrestling is a strenuous sport but one which can be engaged in safely if they follow a proper training routine. "Superman" qualities are unnecessary; any normal boy who possesses the desire and determination can learn to wrestle. There are many notable cases of young men developing into national champions who started wrestling only for the physical purpose of building up their bodies. However, no one should be deluded into believing that success can be achieved in wrestling without an immense amount of hard work.

The importance of warming up before engaging in wrestling matches; the importance of having all minor cuts, abrasions, pulled muscles, etc., treated promptly; and the necessity of regular and intelligent practice should be made absolutely clear.

There should be no actual wrestling matches for the first two weeks, but only demonstration and execution of certain elementary holds and fundamental maneuvers against passive resistance. During this two weeks' period a great deal of attention should be devoted to fundamentals; how to acquire a comfortable and effective stance; how to set up holds from the standing position by pushing, pulling, and feinting an opponent out of position; how to maintain balance and destroy an opponent's balance by "floating" when in a riding position; how to assume and maintain a good base when in the underneath position on the mat; how to stand up from the underneath position; how to lift with the legs, and how to execute many other fundamental skills as part of the warm-up and conditioning program. During this preliminary period it is well not to spend the entire time on holds from any one particular position. The work must be arranged to offer more or less of a cross-section of the various positions which will result in wrestling, such as Standing, Underneath, Riding, etc. In this way the men will get a better concept of just what wrestling is, learn something of the basic principles, and at the same time be conditioning themselves for more technical work later. Road work, preferably outside running, should be commenced the first day by having the men jog for a half mile or so. This should be increased until they can run two miles at a rather fast pace without feeling stiff and tired the next day. This degree of physical condition should be acquired within two weeks. At this time running may be limited to every second or third day and more strenuous wrestling drills should be held.

Calisthenics and conditioning exercises should also start the first day and continue throughout the entire season. Push-ups, chinning, rope-climbing, bridging, and various exercises for strengthening the trunk, abdominal, and neck muscles are all splendid for developing muscles which are of particular importance in wrestling. Rope-skipping is also excellent for developing body co-ordination, muscular control, timing, and physical poise, in addition to its value as a warm-up exercise. To utilize time, however, it is just as well to devote much of the warm-up period to "push and pull" contests and going through certain fundamental wrestling maneuvers. *Never permit any member of the class to engage in wrestling matches against full resistance* until thoroughly warmed up.

Contrary to popular belief, strength and "bulging biceps" are not the most important assets of a wrestler. As a matter of fact, it is not desirable to develop any muscle abnormally. Special exercises and calisthenics should be engaged in only to the extent of giving all muscles the proper "tone." To go further than this will tend to develop a slower muscular reaction. The most important mechanical factors in wrestling are not abnormal strength and muscle development, but co-ordination, balance, timing, and precision in the execution of holds.

## DEVELOPING A VARSITY TEAM

At the conclusion of the two weeks' program of general instruction and conditioning, the men should start on a more strenuous routine. Not less than five minutes should be devoted at the beginning of the period to warm-up drills. The next fifteen minutes should be devoted to instruction and practice against passive resistance in the execution of holds from one of the wrestling positions. Each hold demonstrated should be drilled upon several times, until it is thoroughly understood and some degree of precision in execution acquired. The following five to ten minutes should be devoted to competition against full resistance from the position in which instruction was given. This competition should be engaged in by the entire class at the same time if the wrestling area is large enough. These contests should start and stop at the sound of the whistle and last not longer than thirty seconds to a minute in duration. To illustrate, if the men were to start wrestling from the standing position, they would have thirty seconds to a minute (from whistle to whistle) to get a Take Down on their partner. However, if instruction had been given on Escapes, the same limited time would be allowed to escape from the underneath position, then the men would alternate their position and the other side be given the same length of time to escape. These "whistle drills" should continue until the men show signs of fatigue or for such time as the instructor deems the particular exercise warrants. A few minutes (but not long enough to permit the men to get cold) should then be given to making corrections and giving instructions on certain important phases of the work in which they have engaged. The remaining half of the period should be devoted to a somewhat similar activity in which instruction and practice is given from another wrestling position. Likewise, this instruction period should be followed by similar "whistle drills." At the conclusion of this instruction period the men should be told how far they are expected to run for that particular day, and the Captain or some other responsible team member assigned to lead them in their running exercise. If the men are to do their running out doors, they must be required to have adequate sweat clothes to obviate the possibility of catching cold.

A routine similar to that suggested above, except for a steady progression in intensity, should be continued for approximately two weeks more. During this third two-weeks period, all of the principal holds that are to be given for the season should be covered and the men allowed ample opportunity to practice them. Throughout the season the daily practice periods should be divided so approximately half of the period is devoted to instruction and practice, using the remainder for work and regular matches between picked members of the team. One week or so before the first meet of the season it is well to have a tournament open to all the candidates. This tournament will give additional information on the relative merits of the members of the squad and may serve as a "try out" for the first meet, but it should not be considered as a "closed issue." It is desirable to have regulation matches in which each starting position must be contested for each week.

Naturally, it is desirable to have the team come to its peak for their most important meet on the schedule. This "most important meet" is usually a wrestling tournament, which is the common method now employed in deciding team as well as individual championships.

In order to develop any hold, it must be practiced over and over again, against different partners and opponents before it can be used spontaneously, with confidence, and precision. It requires time to develop the paths of reflex to the degree necessary that holds can be properly timed and the situation instantly recognized when the most opportune time has arisen for application of a particular hold. It is practically impossible to learn a hold the day before a match, or even the week before, and be able to use it successfully against a worthy opponent in competition. The holds and maneuvers which have been diligently practiced in the early season are the ones which will "pay off" in the big championship tournaments.

*Weight Control*

A weight chart of the type which shows the weight before and after workouts should be kept for each member of the team. The information derived from this chart may be helpful in many respects. It may be of value in determining the individual's weight reducing possibilities, how hard he has been working, whether he is growing, and what his weight classification should be.

It is possible for a boy in good physical condition to lose five pounds, and even as much as ten pounds, by dehydration and diet without any deleterious effect. A normal boy who weighs 150 pounds when in good physical condition can usually take off five pounds rather simply and easily by taking some vigorous exercise while dressed in sweat clothes. Thus, this particular boy would be able to weigh in for the 145 pound class instead of having to wrestle a man five pounds heavier in the 155 pound class. In "making weight" for a meet, it is best to come down to near the exact weight which will be required for the match on the night before the meet. By so doing, two or three pounds of water and nourishment can be taken for the evening meal, which will compensate for the two or three pounds of weight which will be lost through the natural process of respiration and elimination before time for weighing in the next afternoon. Weighing in takes place five hours before meet time. By eating immediately after weighing in, close to normal weight will be again gained before the meet.

Excessive weight reduction can become a vicious practice. In a few isolated cases throughout the country some misguided coaches have permitted reduction to such an extent that it could jeopardize the health of a growing boy. There has been much unwarranted and unintelligent criticism, however, of even slight weight reductions by men who do not understand the mechanics or effects of dehydration for such a limited time as is necessary to weigh in for a wrestling meet. Most coaches have the intelligence to understand the weight that their charges can safely lose and they can also be depended upon to have the welfare of their men so much at heart that they will not take any chance of ruining the health of any of them. It is desirable to have the advice and active assistance of competent medical authority before permitting any great reduction in weight to be made.

*Diet, Sleep and Training*

It is impossible to attain that superb degree of physical condition which is so important in wrestling without a serious and conscientious regard for these three factors. All should be regular. Food should be eaten only at meal time; at least eight hours of sleep should be had, and at the same hours each night; and hard, strenuous, vigorous work-outs should be participated in almost every day. Any well balanced diet is satisfactory to train on. Heavy exercise should not be taken within three hours after a meal. Eating when tired and eating too much should be avoided. A balanced meal three times each day with plenty of fresh vegetables and fruit is important. By having a proper diet, all cells of the body are properly fed and replenished, and there is less likelihood of faulty elimination. It is important to have at least one evacuation each day and this should be controlled by diet instead of resorting to laxatives.

*"Staleness"*

It is quite unusual for anyone to become "stale" in wrestling, but infrequently this does happen. Staleness is a physical condition existing which prevents recuperation from fatigue. A combination of factors usually contributes to this condition. Worry, lack of sleep, improper diet, faulty elimination, etc., may all be at the root of this state of lethargy. The symptoms of this ailment are listlessness and a rundown, perpetually tired feeling. Very often, however, what is believed to be "staleness" is nothing more than the result of excessive work done before good physical condition is acquired. If this condition does occur, a day or two lay-off from work, accompanied with plenty of sleep and proper food, will correct it.

## DEVELOPMENT OF A PHYSICAL TRAINING CLASS OR SQUADRON TEAM

In the development of a squadron team, or any unit used in competition in our Naval Aviation Wrestling Program, a much more concentrated routine must be followed. Time prevents the long conditioning program which is used in the development of a varsity team. The same general plan should be followed, however, with fewer holds and less technique being taught. Good physical condition must be assumed and a more rapid advancement is necessary. Only basic fundamentals should be taught and more work required in preparing the cadets for the Sports Program contests. Each cadet should first be given the minimum maneuvers to enable him to win a match. There should be a steady progression.

# CHAPTER VI
# Take Downs and Counters

A great deal of latitude should be given to allow for individual differences and peculiarities in determining the stance which a wrestler should assume in a standing position. Generally speaking, any position can be assumed which allows freedom of movement and permits application of "pet" holds which have been perfected. However, before a stance is accepted, careful consideration must be given to the question of whether it offers an adequate defense for countering or blocking the more common holds used from the standing position, whether it provides a good base, and whether it permits maneuverability.

### Stance

Most good wrestlers have one foot slightly forward, with the feet spread from eighteen to twenty-four inches, weight resting on the balls of the feet, knees slightly bent and the whole body relaxed to the greatest possible degree.

Slightly advancing one foot has been used advantageously by many wrestlers to bait an opponent into a favorable position for execution of a favorite hold or counter-hold.

For convenience and simplicity all holds will be described with "A" executing the hold against "B." The illustrations are in contrasting colors showing "A" dressed in a black uniform and "B" dressed in a white uniform.

All holds described will be shown from only one side. Obviously, they can be executed from either the right or left side. To illustrate, in all Leg Tackles, Drags, Arm Locks, etc., the illustrations will show "A" attacking "B's" right side. "B's" left side can be attacked in the same manner by substituting right for left and left for right in the descriptions of the holds. This same method will be followed in illustrating and describing holds from the positions on the mat. In describing holds to be used in "Escaping from Underneath," it will be assumed that "B" is "Riding" on "A's" left side and in describing "Break Downs" and "Rides," it will be assumed that "A" is operating from "B's" left side.

# TAKE DOWNS AND COUNTERS

*The Open Stance*

1—Any comfortable position can be assumed which lends itself to maneuverability and provides a convenient base for initiating the holds which have been adapted to a particular style of wrestling.

*The Closed Stance*

2—From a closed stance there can be any number of "locked" positions. The position to be assumed should be one to suit the convenience and style of the individual.

**Setting Up a Single or Double Leg Tackle**

The preliminary moves which can be used in securing a leg hold are infinite. Any push, pull, fake, or feint that will cause your opponent to expose his leg or legs can be employed. Body control, speed, timing, and precision of execution are of the utmost importance for successful application of any hold. The following ten pictures [3–12] illustrate methods which may be employed.

3—Head lead and push

4—Head lead and pull

5—*Elbow push up*

6—*Elbow pull down*

7—*Chin push*

8—*Arm bend pull down*

9—*Fake arm drag*

10—*Under arm drag*

11—"Tie up" and push away

12—Spinning on hand from a football crouch

### The Single Leg Tackle

This should not be considered as an isolated hold but rather as several methods of procedure that may be followed after you have maneuvered your opponent into a position where he has provided you with an opportunity to grab one of his legs. The reaction of your opponent then determines which method you should follow to complete a Take Down. All methods should be considered together and practiced to make your selection automatic and spontaneous. This whole series of Leg Tackles should be considered as being based upon general principles and not as specific methods of executing the maneuvers in the exact order as illustrated. This is a clear example of "chain wrestling." It must be understood that any and all of the maneuvers can be used in any combination that is desired if the situation is right for it. We have already noted ten methods of initiating or "setting up" this hold. There are many others. In considering the secondary problem of completing a Take Down there are several principles common to all of the methods to be shown which should be adhered to. They are:

1. Time properly in following up after your initial maneuver.
2. Push off of your back foot when starting your drive forward to secure opponent's leg.
3. Drive your head to the pit of your opponent's stomach.
4. Spin toward the leg being attacked.
5. *Drive deeply and hard with knees well under your body to maintain a good base.*
6. Follow up quickly with a hard, quick pull before your opponent has time to recover.

*Head Lead and Push.*—Completed with a Double Leg Snap.

13a—A places his right hand on B's neck and grasps B's right elbow with his left hand. A leads B forward, pushes B's head to B's right with the heel of A's right hand, thereby making B expose his left leg.

13b—A drops deeply, pivots on his left hand, grasps B's left knee with the crook of his right arm.

13c—A completes a Go Behind by encircling both of B's legs with his arms and pulling B down.

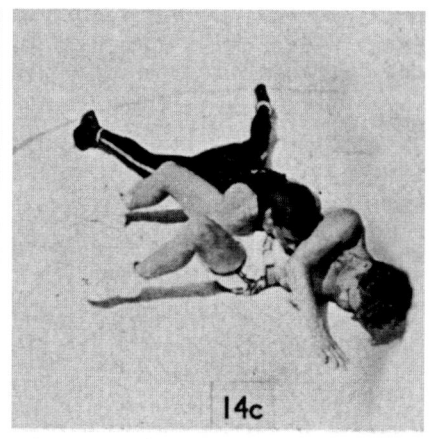

*Head Lead and Pull.*—Completed with a Single Leg Snap.

14a—With same lock as described in the preceding maneuver, A leads B forward in same manner but instead of pushing, A pulls B's head with his right hand, thereby exposing B's right leg.

14b—A swings to his left, drives deeply and grasps B's right knee with the crook of his left arm. A grasps B's right heel with his right hand, drives his head upward into the pit of B's stomach, and brings B backward on his buttocks.

14c—A drives into B and secures an Inside Crotch hold with his right arm.

*Chin Push.*—Completed by Using a Back Heel.

Again it is assumed that A has the same lock as was described in the first maneuver. But this time assume that B is a "strong-armed" boy who locks tightly in this "tied-up" position.

>15a—A reaches over B's right arm and pushes against B's chin with the heel of his left hand. This will expose B's right leg.
>
>15b—A drops deeply, pivots on his right hand, grasps B's right knee with the crook of his left arm.
>
>15c—A completes a Go Behind by hooking his left heel behind B's right heel. A reaches his right hand in behind B's left knee, pulls with his left leg and forces B to the mat on his buttocks. A drives into B and secures an Inside Crotch hold with his right arm.

*Fake Arm Drag.*—Completed with a Double Ankle Pull.

>16a—From either an open or closed stance, A grasps B's right wrist with his left hand. A hooks under B's right armpit with his right hand. A gives a short, quick pull on B's right arm, making B expose his right leg.
>
>16b—A releases B's arm, drives in with his head to the pit of B's stomach, plants his right hand on the mat, and encircles B's right leg with his left arm.

16c—A gives a quick pull with his left arm, swings behind B, grasps B's insteps with both hands.

16d—A drives B to the mat to complete a Go Behind.

*Spinning on Hand from a Football Crouch.*—Completed by a Head Lift.

17a—From an open stance, A drops on his right hand and right knee in a crouched position.

17b—A pivots on his right hand, swings to his left, and hooks behind B's right knee with the crook of his left arm.

17c—A pulls with his left arm, lifts with his head, catches under B's left thigh with his right hand, brings his right foot up, and drives B in a circular motion over onto his buttocks.

17d—A follows up with an Inside Crotch hold. (To become proficient in the use of this maneuver, it is necessary to employ a bit of finesse. You must be able to spin on either hand, making possible an attack on either of your opponent's legs. Especially must you be able to change from a crouch on your right knee and right hand to one on your left knee and left hand, and vice versa. This hold is made particularly effective by faking an attack against your opponent's right leg and then quickly changing to your left hand and left knee for an attack on his left leg.)

*The Double Leg Tackle*

18a—This is set up by any of the methods previously suggested on pages 23 and 24.

18b—A drops in deeply on both knees, drives hard, and pulls downward on B's left knee.

18c—A lifts with his head, comes up on his left foot, drives B in a circular motion to B's left over onto his buttocks.

18d—A maintains control by keeping his weight properly distributed.

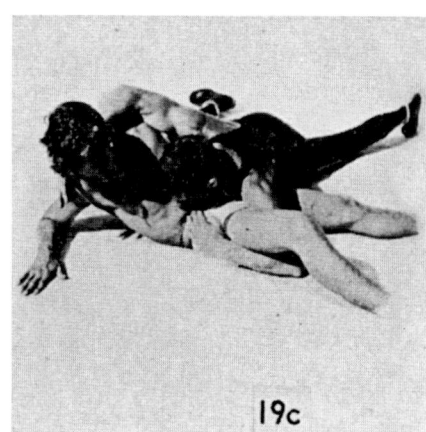

**Double Leg Pick Up and Back Heel**

19a—This hold can be set up by any of the previously suggested methods on pages 23 and 24.

19b—As in the preceding hold, A drops in deeply on both knees, pulls hard on B's left knee with his right arm, and steps behind B's left foot with his right foot.

19c—A drives with his head, which is on the right side of B's body, scoops with his right foot, and drives B backward onto his buttocks. A follows up with an Inside Crotch hold.

# TAKE DOWNS AND COUNTERS

***The Double Leg Tackle, Pick Up, Crotch, and Half Nelson***

20a—From a locked position, A grasps B's right wrist with his left hand, drops to his right knee, and ducks his head under B's right arm.

20b—A secures an Inside Crotch, lifts B, and comes to a standing position.

20c—A swings B at right angles to his chest while securing a deep Half Nelson with his right arm.

20d—A drops to his right knee, placing B's shoulders on the mat while retaining this most effective pin hold.

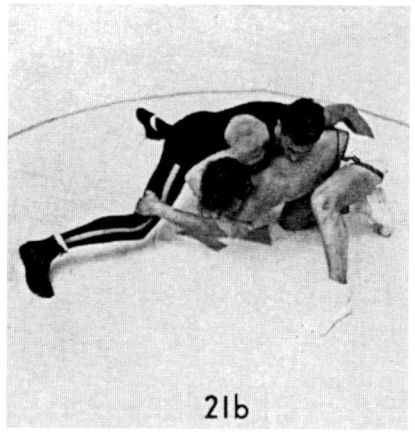

### Counters for Leg Tackles and Leg Pick Ups
*Cross Face*

21a—A drives his legs backward, catching under B's arms to block B's direct attack.

21b—A applies a cross face with his right hand and grabs B's buttocks with his left hand.

21c—A grasps B's right ankle while spinning behind.

*Whizzer (Over Arm Hook)*

22—A hooks over B's left arm (if A's right leg is being attacked), pulls upward, and drops his left foot backward so that the line of direction of A's feet will form a "T" with the line of direction of B's feet. (This hold is described in detail on page 44.)

*Reverse Thigh and Far Elbow*

23a—A spreads his feet, shoots his legs backward, reaches over B's right arm with his left arm, and grabs inside of B's right thigh.

23b—A grasps B's left elbow with his right hand, lifts up on B's thigh with his left hand, and in a circular motion pulls B over onto his back.

# TAKE DOWNS AND COUNTERS

*Snap Down*

24a—A places his right hand on the back of B's neck and with his left hand grasps behind B's right upper arm.

24b—A drops his right leg backward and at the same time gives B a quick pull, forcing him to the mat.

24c—A quickly hops behind B before he has time to recover.

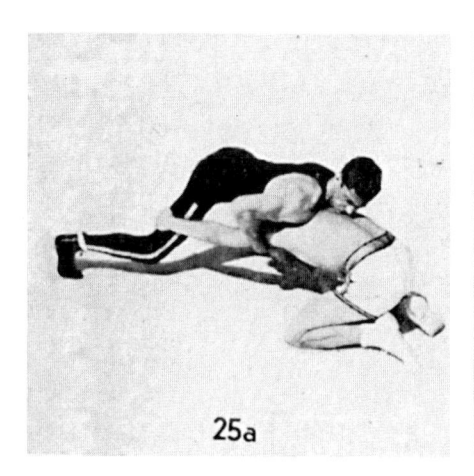

*Reverse Quarter Nelson*

25a—A spreads his feet and shoots his legs backward.

25b—A places his right hand on the back of B's neck, reaches over B's right arm with his left arm, and grasps his own right wrist. A now has a Reverse Quarter Nelson.

25c—A forces B's head down, pries him over onto his left side, then spins around into a Reverse Half Nelson and Crotch Hold or Cradle.

*Single Arm Drag*

26a—A grabs B's right wrist with his left hand and hooks under B's right arm with his right hand.

26b—A pulls upward on B's arm and swings him to the mat.

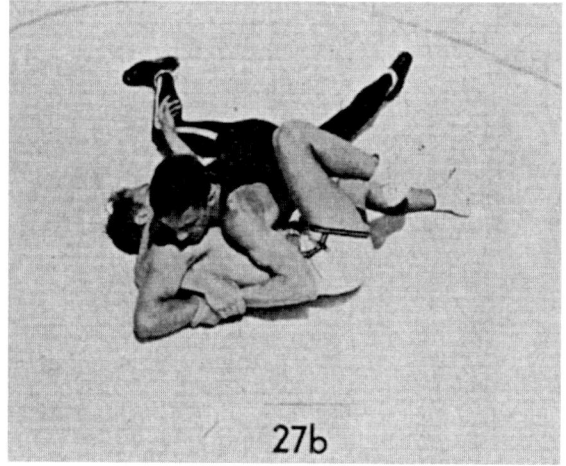

*Double Wrist Lock*

27a—A grasps B's right wrist with his left hand, reaches over B's right arm with his right arm, and grasps his own wrist. A now has a Double Wrist Lock.

27b—A gives a violent jerk upward, forcing B over onto his back. (This hold is described in detail on page 47.)

### Crotch Lift and Back Heel

A sets this up by any of the methods illustrated in securing a Leg Tackle. (See pages 23 and 24.)

> 28a—This time A does not drop to his knees; instead, he steps deeply to B's right side, takes an Inside Crotch hold with his hands locked around B's right leg in a "wrestler's grip." (This grip is similar to the car coupling lock of a train. It is the only method to be used when clasping your hands.)
>
> 28b—A steps behind B's right foot with his left foot, drives with his left shoulder, catches under B's left thigh with his right hand, and Back Heels B to the mat.
>
> 28c—A comes into an Inside Crotch hold as B is brought to the mat.

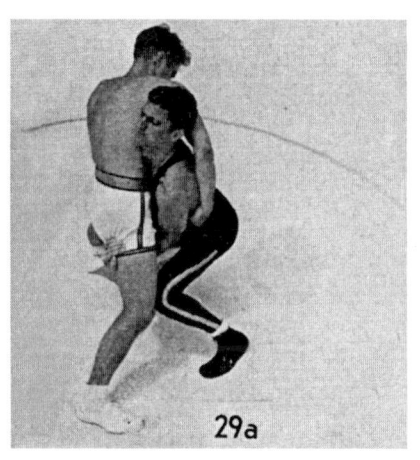

### Crotch Lift and Half Nelson

> 29a—A obtains a crotch hold in the same manner as was described in the preceding hold, but instead of using a Back Heel, A lifts B. (Be sure to always lift with your legs and not with your back.)
>
> 29b—A takes a deep Inside Crotch hold with his left hand and, as B is lifted, secures a Half Nelson with his right arm.
>
> 29c—A drops on his right knee, bringing B to the mat, and retains this hold for a fall.

### Counters for a Crotch Lift

*Reverse Thigh and Far Elbow.*—(See page 32.)

*Arm Tie Up and Hip Throw*

>30a—A hooks his left arm over and around B's right arm and grabs B's left elbow with his right hand.
>
>30b—A extends his left leg backward in order to break B's grip.
>
>30c—A grasps B's left wrist with his right hand, steps in front of B's left leg, and trips B to the mat.
>
>30d—A retains B's arms in this locked position to secure a fall.

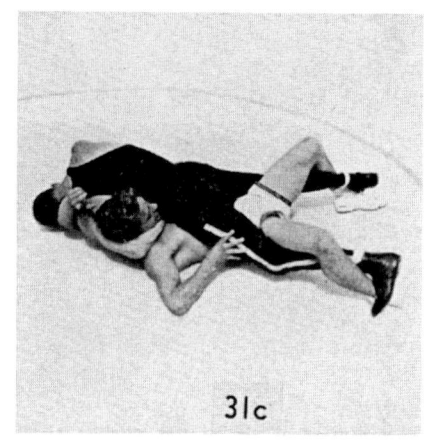

### Head Under Arm and Back Heel

31a—A grabs B's left wrist with his right hand, pulls outward, and at the same time drives his head under B's left arm.

31b—A lifts with his head, swings his left leg in behind B's right leg, and pulls with a Back Heel, forcing B to the mat on his buttocks.

31c—A follows up with a Double Grapevine.

### Head Under Arm Sneak

32a—A grips the back of B's neck with his right hand and grasps B's right wrist with his left hand. A forces the top of his head against B's right clavicle.

32b—A jerks B forward, drops on his right knee, and drives his head under B's right arm. A drives upward, keeping a "bull-neck," and goes behind B.

32c—A encircles B's waist with his left arm and secures a wrestler's grip. A brings B to the mat by any of the methods suggested in Chapter VIII. (This hold is simple but very effective if properly timed.)

## Head Under Arm Series

The next three holds represent an interesting sequence. They should be taught together as alternative maneuvers. This is another clear example of what is meant by "chain wrestling."

### Head Under Arm and Crotch Lift

33a—A reaches over B's left arm with his right arm, grasps above B's left elbow with his right hand and B's neck with his left hand.

33b—A jerks simultaneously on B's neck and arm and drops deeply under B on both of his knees. A grabs inside of B's left thigh with his left arm, retains a tight grip on B's left elbow, and drives his head up under B's left arm.

33c—A swings B free of the mat.

33d—A brings B onto his back.

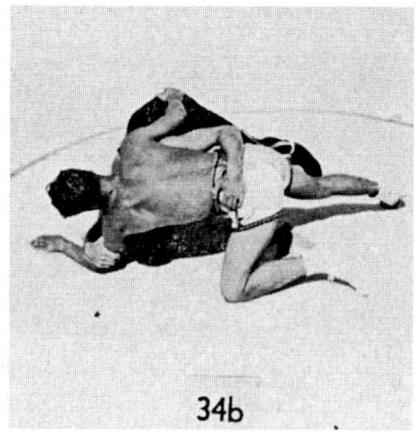

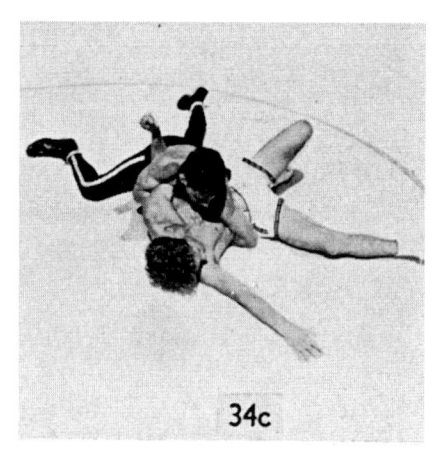

## Head Under Arm and Arm Pull

34a—Assume that the preceding hold is attempted but cannot be completed because B has shot his legs backward and flattened himself out.

34b—In this event, A gives a quick pull on B's left elbow, pulls B forward in a line parallel to B's body, and brings his left hand up over B's back and pulls B under him.

34c—A fall is secured with an Arm Bar and Body Lock.

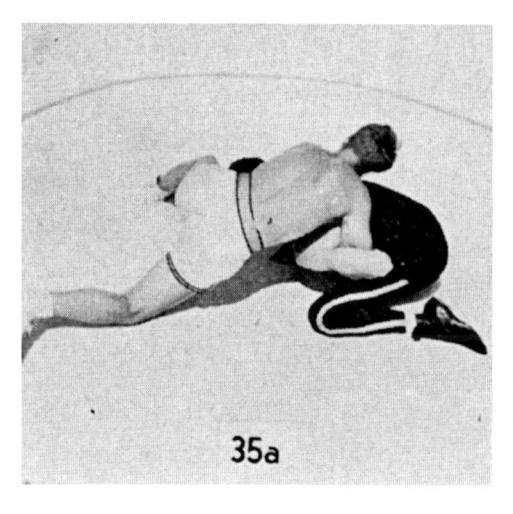

## The Double Arm Lock and Roll

35a—Let us again make the same supposition as in the preceding illustration. But this time B has reached over A's left arm. A locks B's right elbow tightly in the crook of his left arm.

35b—A drives and lifts under B's left arm, and wing-locks to B's right side.

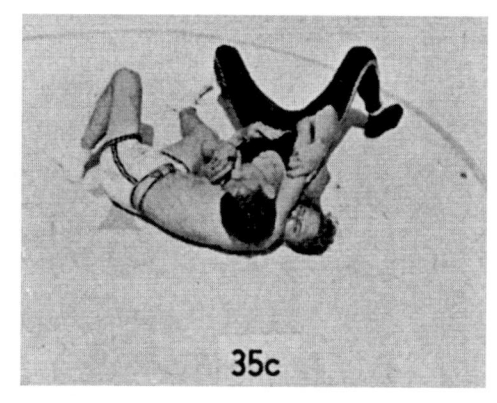

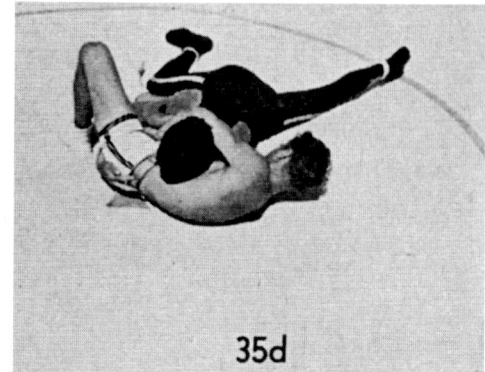

35c—It is possible for A to pin B with this hold by retaining a double arm lock and keeping his weight properly distributed.

35d—If A feels his arm slipping, he will turn toward B's legs, preferably into an Inside Crotch hold, to complete a Go Behind. (It is a cardinal principle to always turn toward your opponent's legs.)

**Counters for Head Under Arm Situations**

*Cross Face.*—(See page 32.)
*Reverse Thigh and Far Elbow.*—(See page 32.)
*Whizzer.*—(See page 44.)

**Head Under Arm Spin**

36a—A works into a locked up position. A overhooks B's left arm, taking a firm grip with his right hand above B's left elbow. A feints an attack to B's left leg.

36b—A shifts his head from under B's left shoulder to a position under B's right shoulder, lifts with his head, and steps deeply with his right foot between B's feet.

36c—A grasps the hock of B's right knee with his left hand, pulls downward in a circular motion on B's left arm, and brings B to the mat.

# TAKE DOWNS AND COUNTERS

### *The Merry Go Round*

37a—A places his right hand on B's neck and drives with his head against B's right shoulder. A maneuvers B into position, by pulling and pushing, so that B will expose his right leg.

37b—A drops to his right knee, pulls down on B's head, and grasps with his left hand behind the hock of B's right knee.

37c—A lifts on B's leg and pulls down on B's head in a circular motion to bring B to the mat.

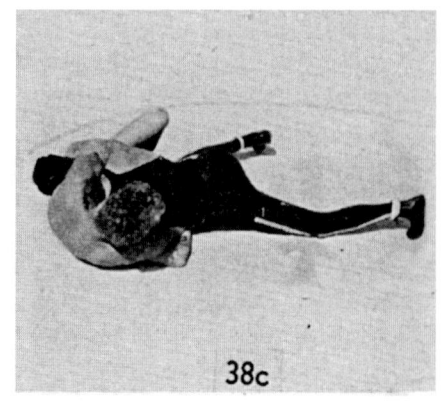

*The Double Arm Lock*

This is a dangerous hold when used from a standing position. The purpose of including it is for a precaution against having it worked on you.

38a—A reaches with his right hand over B's left arm grasping above B's elbow. A drives his head under B's left arm, and grasps B's right wrist with his left hand in a reverse manner (with his thumb toward the extremity of B's hand). A hooks his left elbow underneath the crook of B's right arm.

38b—A pulls tightly, lifts up, pivots on his right foot, and swings his left leg through, which will crash B's head to the mat.

38c—A rolls toward B's legs to complete the Go Behind.

## Counter for a Double Arm Lock
## Never Permit Opponent to Lock Both Arms

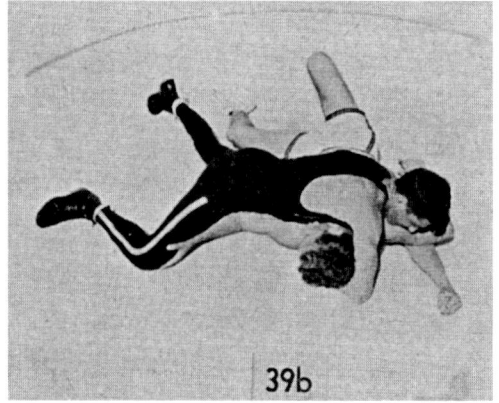

*Head Chancery and Bar Arm*

This hold is also used quite commonly as a counter for Leg Tackles, but it can be initiated by maneuvering to get your opponent's head lower than your shoulder.

39a—A encircles B's neck with his right arm and grasps B's chin with his right hand. With his left hand, A pulls up under B's right shoulder, and drops to his right knee.

39b—A pulls B in a circular motion until B's shoulders are pressed to the mat.

# TAKE DOWNS AND COUNTERS

*Counter for Head Chancery and Bar Arm*
  *Head Under Arm Series.*—(See page 38.)

*Double Bar Arm Lock*
  40a—A drives both of his arms inside and under B's arms with B's neck under A's right armpit. A keeps his feet spread and well back so B will be forced to carry A's weight. A quickly pulls up under B's arms and locks his fingers in a wrestler's grip behind B's back.
  40b—A sits down, brings his left foot under B's right thigh, elevates, and carries B onto his back.
  40c—A secures a fall with the Bar Lock and Double Grapevine.

*Block for Double Bar Arm Lock*
  Lock hands and lift with your head to prevent him from getting his hands locked. Then proceed to one of Head Under Arm Series (see page 38).

*Counter for Double Bar Arm Lock*
  *Reverse Thigh and Far Elbow.*—(See page 32.)

**Whizzer Series** (Over Arm Hook Variations)

This represents an important series of "chain wrestling" holds. For the most part, the determining factor as to which maneuver to be used is the position of your opponent's feet.

*Hip Lock*

    41a—A maneuvers B into a position which will enable him to place his left arm over B's right arm.

    41b—A grasps B's left elbow with his right hand and locks B's upper right arm in the crook of his left arm.

    41c—A steps across deeply in front of B, lifts with his left arm, and pulls B down (in a circular motion) with his right hand.

    41d—A brings B underneath onto his back in a pinning position.

*Fast Lateral Drop*

    42a—From the same locked position as described in the preceding hold, assume B is pushing or steps back with his right foot.

    42b—In that event, A reaches deeply under B's left shoulder with his right arm. A grips B's right upper arm with his left hand, straightens his left leg, and drives his left foot against B's right foot.

    42c—A pulls B in a circular motion onto his back.

    42d—A shifts to a perpendicular position to secure a fall.

*Slow Lateral Drop*

43a—A reaches under B's left arm with his right arm around B's back. A's left arm over-hooks B's right arm, grasping above B's right elbow.

43b—A drops to his knees in this locked position, thereby enticing B to follow.

43c—A comes back to a standing position. As B starts to get to his feet, A shifts his feet from a line parallel to one which is perpendicular to B's feet. A pulls down on B's right arm, lifts under B's left shoulder, drops to his right knee, and pulls B forward in a circular motion onto B's back.

45d—A retains this same locked hold for a fall.

*Arm Lock and Heel Pick Up*

44a—From the same locked position as used in the three preceding holds, assume that A starts to Hip Lock by stepping in front of B with his left foot.

44b—If B's right foot is exposed, A reaches between his own legs and grasps B's right heel.

44c—From this position, A pulls upward on B's heel, sits down, and holds B securely with this lock for a fall. (Reverse Jack Knife.) A fourth possibility is that your opponent spreads his feet, shoots his legs back, and starts flattening himself out. In this event, use either the Reverse Thigh and Far Elbow Lock (see page 32) or the Reverse Quarter Nelson (see page 33).

**Counters for Whizzer Holds**

*Crotch Lift.*—(See page 35.)

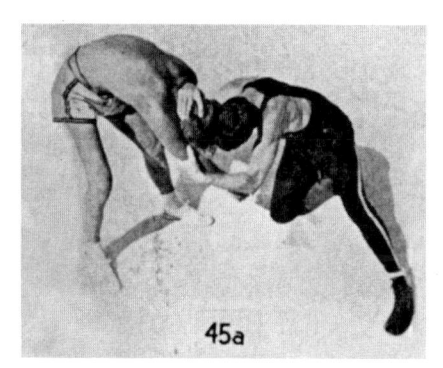

*Head and Far Heel Pick Up*

45a—A grasps with his right hand on B's neck, and with his left hand grasps B's right elbow. A leads B forward, pushes with the heel of his right hand, which causes B to expose his left foot.

45b—A drops to his right knee, releases his left hand from B's right elbow, and grabs B's left heel with his left hand.

45c—A pulls on B's heel and simultaneously drives downward and backward on B's neck with his right hand, which forces B to the mat on his buttocks.

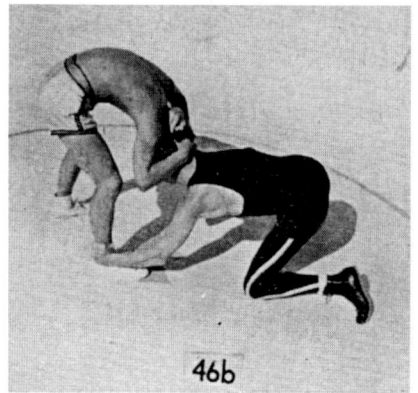

*Head and Near Heel Pick Up*

Either of B's heels may be attacked. If B's left leg is exposed more than his right, A may proceed in this manner:

> 46a—Instead of A pushing with his right hand, he may pull, thereby causing B to expose his right foot.
>
> 46b—In this event, A grabs B's right heel and drives with his right hand.
>
> 46c—Heavy pressure should be exerted and maintained upon B's neck while pulling upward on B's heel.

*Block for Head and Heel Pick Up*

Keep a firm grip on your opponent's neck with your elbow in and against his chest. Keep your feet well spread and back.

*Single Arm Drag*

Some knowledge of the operation and possibilities from this situation is essential for the finished wrestler. The variations relating to this hold are many. As is true in most holds, perhaps all, the most important thing is "setting it up," recognizing the situation when it can be used appropriately, and executing it quickly before your opponent has sensed what you intend to do. Below are three methods for setting up an arm drag.

> 47—A fakes a leg pick up from an open distance, making B reach out his arms to block.

# TAKE DOWNS AND COUNTERS

48—From a closed stance, A drives outward against B's forearm, thereby opening up an opportunity to grasp B's wrist.

49—From a closed stance, A transfers his head from B's left shoulder to B's right. A grasps B's right wrist with his left hand and proceeds with a Drag. (This is a very, subtle maneuver and was used repeatedly by one of the greatest exponents of the Arm Drag.)

In its simplest aspect, the hold is secured in the following manner:

50a—A grasps B's right wrist with his left hand and quickly slides his right hand under B's right armpit.

50b—A guides B's right arm across in front of his body with his left hand, jerks quickly with his right hand, and simultaneously steps between B's legs with his right foot. A keeps his right leg straight as he drops to his right buttocks and pulls B to the mat.

50c—Before B hits the mat, A's left hand should be disengaged from B's right wrist and brought to B's right knee to be used as an aid to the right arm in pulling B down. It also prevents B from using a Cross Body Block, which is a very popular and common counter employed against the Arm Drag. After A has pulled B to the mat, he must make a quick recovery and pull himself behind B.

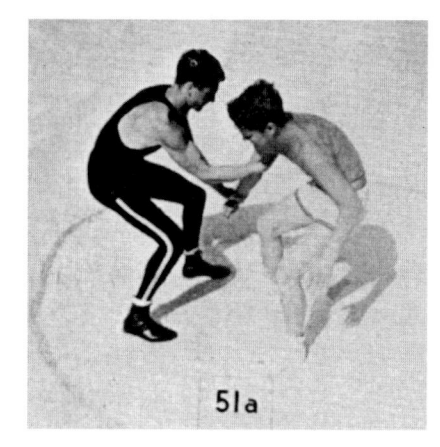

*Pulling Trip*

51a—This is an excellent variation of an Arm Drag. It is fundamentally the same hold as described above.

51b—A uses his right foot to kick B's right foot at the precise instant A starts the Drag.

51c—A proceeds from this point in identical manner as before. Perfect timing is necessary for the execution of this hold.

*Arm Drag with Inside Back Heel*

52a—This is a perfect hold when B resists by bracing his leg (even slightly). A bit of experimentation may first be indulged in to determine what B's reaction may be.

52b—In this maneuver, instead of A pulling B to the mat, he gives an upward pull under B's arm, retains his grasp on B's wrist, and steps in with his right foot for an inside Back Heel behind B's right leg.

52c—Care must be exercised in weight distribution to prevent B from re-dragging. This hold requires finesse, a good sense of balance, co-ordination, and timing.

*Arm Jerk Go Behind*

53a—A secures B's arm in the same manner, but instead of pulling B to the mat, A swings behind.

53b—A locks his hands around B's waist in a wrestler's grip. Methods of taking an opponent to the mat from this position will be discussed thoroughly in Chapter VIII.

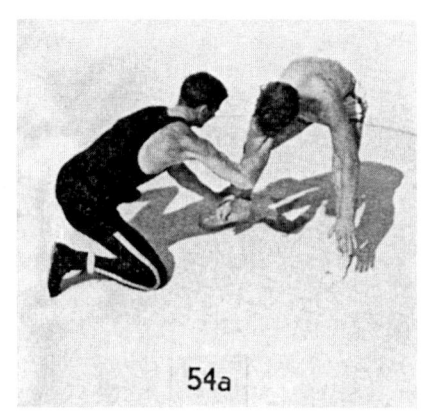

*Arm Drag and Heel Pick Up*

54a—Again, execution of this hold must depend upon what your opponent does. If B braces with his right foot, A relinquishes his grasp on B's wrist and grasps B's heel with his left hand.

54b—A drives his right elbow into B's groin as he pulls up on B's heel.

54c—A forces B backward to the mat on his buttocks. (It will be noted that a little different technique in the execution of the Drag is shown here. Many coaches use this method exclusively. That is, they drop to their inside knee as they start the Drag instead of driving the inside foot in between opponent's legs. If your opponent does not brace with his right foot, it is probable that he can be taken on to the mat with the Drag.)

## Counters for Single Arm Drag

*Cross Body Block*

55a—At the same instant B starts his pull on A's right arm, A drives across B's body, hooks his right heel behind B's left knee.

55b—A pulls hard with a Back Heel, forcing B to the mat on B's buttocks. A takes an Inside Crotch hold with his left arm.

*Re-Drag*

56a—When B takes A's right arm for a Drag, A will find that he has precisely the same opportunity to Drag B.

56b—As B starts his Drag on A, A goes with it but continues with a Drag of his own, swinging on through and behind B after he has pulled B to the mat.

56c—A comes into top position by Scissoring B's leg and pulling through on B's arm.

*Double Wrist Lock*

This hold, when used from the standing position, is employed chiefly as a counter for a Leg Pick-Up. But it can be initiated by setting it up.

57a—A grasps B's right wrist with his left hand and reaches over B's right upper arm with his right hand grasping his own left wrist.

57b—A keeps B's right arm bent in this lock which has been secured, pulls B forward, and drops on his own right knee.

57c—Just as A's knee hits the mat, he jerks hard on B's right arm and forces it upward behind B's back. A drives into B, keeps perpendicular to him, and forces him over onto his back. A keeps his weight centered on B's chest.

Warning: The rules require that the force must be applied at an angle which is parallel to the long axis of the body.

*Block for a Double Wrist Lock*

A clasps his own hands together and pulls upward, thereby breaking Double Wrist Lock.

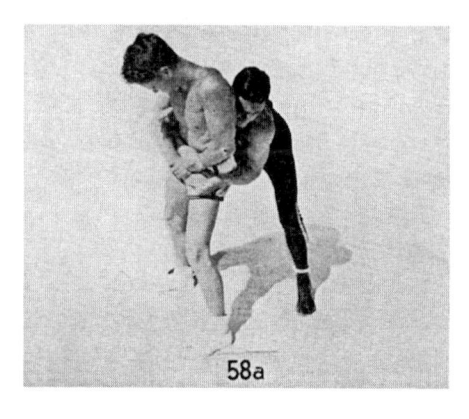

*Counter for a Double Wrist Lock*

58a—A uses his free arm (left) to encircle B's waist, gripping his hands together.

58b—A lifts B, sweeps with his right foot against B's right foot, and drops B on his right shoulder. (In using this Counter, be sure to drop opponent to the same side on which the Double Wrist Lock is being applied. If you inadvertently drop him on the other side, he can still put on a Double Wrist Lock just as he hits the mat. The Double Wrist Lock is a dangerous hold and likewise the counter is very severe. It can result in breaking your opponent's arm or dislocating his clavicle. Extreme caution should be exercised.)

### Side Head Lock

Every unskilled wrestler is apt to use this hold, which is a favorite hold in European wrestling. There have been a number of effective variations developed for securing this hold. However, most American coaches do not use it because the Counters are considered more effective than is the Side Head Lock.

Only one Side Head Lock is illustrated here and, strictly speaking, it is not exactly a Head Lock. The principle purpose of presenting it is in order that we may consider the Counters for it.

> 59a—With his left hand A grasps B's right arm just above B's right elbow. A encircles B's head with his right arm and with his right hand grasps B's upper arm at his right armpit. A steps deeply with his right foot in front of B.
> 59b—A pulls B over his back in a circular motion to the mat. A retains this hold if possible for a pin. If B begins to slip, A bridges into him and rolls toward B's legs to complete a Go Behind.

### Counters for Side Headlock
*Backward Drop*

60a—A drops his right hand to the bend behind B's right knee.

60b—A lifts and falls backward, bringing B onto his back.

60c—A rolls toward B's legs and secures an Inside Crotch hold. (If B retains his Head Lock after he hits the mat, A lifts with his head, pivots on his chest, swings to B's left side, and applies a Half Nelson for a fall.)

*Forward Trip*

61a—The Counter, *which should discourage the use of a Head Lock*, is for A to lift upward on B, and sweep B's right foot out from under him.

61b—A crashes B to the mat. (This Counter may cause serious damage to your opponent and, of course, should be used with extreme caution.)

CHAPTER VII

# Go Behind from Head On

Many wrestlers prefer to work from their knees when in a neutral position. This is referred to as the "Head On" position. It is a somewhat more conservative position than to be on your feet, in that you are not as vulnerable to Leg Pick Ups and you also have a more substantial base from which to operate. However, your maneuverability is restricted and the possibilities of attack are much more limited. It is imperative that every wrestler learn how to cope with this situation. Even though it may not be the purpose of either you or your opponent to work from this position, the natural course of the match may lead to it. Naturally, the one having the better knowledge of methods of attack will have an advantage when this situation does occur.

"Top Side," that is, keeping your opponent's head under your chest or arms, is usually considered better than the "Down Under" position. Possibilities of holds for securing a Go Behind are greater and you have the important advantage of making your opponent carry your weight when you are operating from the "Top Side."

A bit of reflection will make it apparent that most holds described and illustrated as Counters for the Leg Tackles and Leg Pick Up series can be used here by the wrestler occupying the "Top Side" position. And it should be brought to your attention that those holds described in the "Head Under Arm" series from the standing position can be used by the wrestler occupying the "Down Under" position, when you are working "Head On."

*It must be understood that all holds used from the Standing position are capable of being used from the Head On position.* However, some are more feasible than others. For illustration, it has already been noted that a Leg Pick Up or a Leg Tackle is more difficult to get from this position than from standing, because of the more substantial base of your opponent and for the added reason that by dropping to his knees he has already set himself in a good position to protect his legs and counter any attempt to get them.

In order that you may better understand this position, the following illustrations are shown.

# TAKE DOWNS AND COUNTERS

*Head On Position*

62a—This illustration shows A in the Top Side and B in the Down Under position.

62b—This illustration shows another normal Head On situation in which the contestants are sparring for an opening.

There are some holds which are peculiarly applicable from the Head On position, and which are not feasible from standing. The following holds can be used effectively from this position.

*Go Behinds from Top Side*

*Whizzer Series.*—(See page 44.)
*Reverse Quarter Nelson.*—(See page 33.)
*Bar Arm and Head Chancery.*—(See page 42.)
*Reverse Thigh and Far Elbow.*—(See page 32.)
*Snap Down.*—(See page 33.)

*Short Arm Drag.*—(See also page 48.)

63a—It will be noted that B's hand has been "trapped" to the mat immediately preceding the start of the Drag.

63b—A keeps B's left hand trapped while executing a Drag.

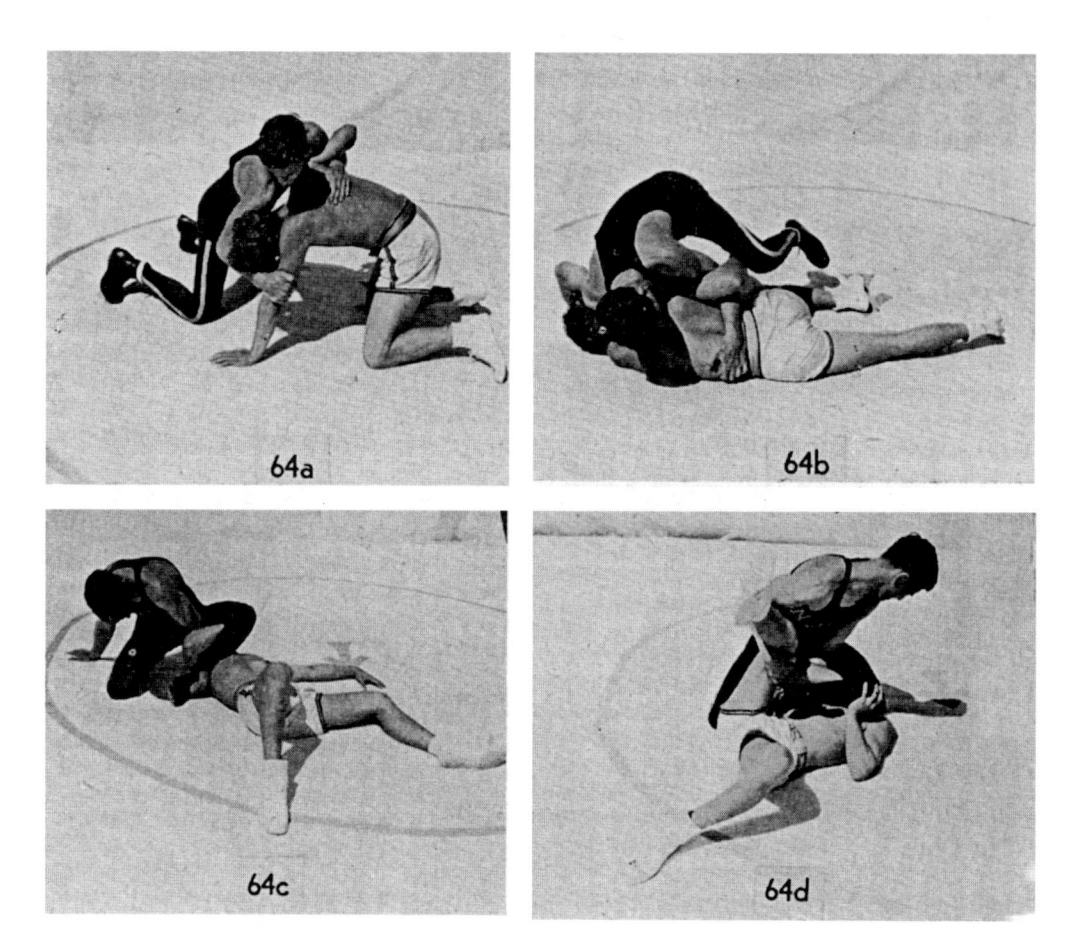

*Short Arm Scissors*

64a—A grasps B's left elbow with his right hand and hooks under B's right arm with his left arm.

64b—A pulls B forward onto his left shoulder by pulling simultaneously on B's left arm and lifting under his right shoulder.

64c—A steps over B's body with his left leg, grasps his own left ankle (keeping B's left arm locked in the vice thus created), and pivots on his left foot with his left knee pressed into B's chest.

64d—A grasps below the knee of B's right leg, which will assist in maintaining A's balance and also in securing B's shoulders to the mat for a fall.

## Go Behinds from Down Under

From the Down Under position, any of the Head Under Arm series which were illustrated from the Standing position, are appropriate. (See page 38.)

*Single Leg Tackle.*—Completed with a Head Lift. (See page 28.)
*Single Leg Tackle.*—Completed with a Back Heel. (See page 27.)
*Double Leg Tackle.*—Completed with a Head Lift. (See page 29.)

CHAPTER VIII

# Taking to Mat from Standing

There are many situations that may develop during the course of a wrestling match in which you find yourself behind your opponent, or your opponent behind you, with both of you in the standing position.

When starting in a neutral position, you are not awarded points for obtaining a Take Down by merely going behind your opponent. You must bring him on down to the mat in a position of control.

This situation occurs more frequently perhaps when your opponent stands up in attempting to escape from the underneath position and you have followed him up with your arms locked around his waist from the rear.

*Standing Rear Body Lock*

65—A's right arm encircles B's waist with hands locked in a wrestler's grip over B's left groin. A keeps his head (right ear) pressed against B's back with his feet spread and back. A keeps B under control by keeping his arms locked tightly and moving B forward and backward.

From this position A brings B to the mat by one of the following methods:

*Back Heel*

66a—A drives his left foot against B's left heel, keeping his left leg straight and kicking B's left foot out from under him.

66b—A pulls B to the mat in a circular motion, retains a Body Lock, and forces B down into a prone position on the mat by driving his right shoulder into the small of B's back.

*The Leg Sweep.*—This maneuver subjects an opponent to rather rough treatment, when properly timed. The rules require that you drop to one knee before slamming your opponent to the mat. But even when conforming to this rule, it is still possible to give your opponent a severe jolt.

67a—A steps between B's legs with his right foot, lifts and "sweeps" with his left foot against the outside of B's left foot.
67b—A drives into B to prevent him recovering.
67c—A obtains a Bar Lock on B's left arm.

*The Forward Trip*

68a—This picture illustrates a different lock around B's waist, known as a "Two on One" Bar Lock. A steps between B's legs with his right foot, lifts and trips B forward with his left leg encircling B's left leg.

68b—A retains the Bar Lock and distributes his weight for better leverage.

*Far Elbow and Rear Crotch Lift.*—This is another maneuver which deals quite severely with your opponent.

69a—A grasps above B's right elbow with his left hand and B's left thigh from the rear with his right hand.

69b—A lifts and drives B to the mat on his right shoulder. As B hits the mat, A attempts to follow up and secure a fall with a cradle or some other Pinning Combination.

*Ankle Snap and Leg Trip*

    70a—B grasps A's hands preventing A from locking around B's waist.

    70b—A jerks his left hand loose, grasps B's left ankle with his left hand, lifts and drives his right leg between B's legs, and trips him forward.

CHAPTER IX

# Escapes from Standing

*It is important to realize that most escapes that can be used from the underneath position when down on the mat can also be used from a standing position when your opponent is behind.* Escapes will be described and illustrated in detail in Chapter XII. There are some holds, however, which can be used much more effectively from a standing position than from down on the mat.

The following four holds are suggested as being particularly feasible as escapes from this Standing position:

**Standing Rear Body Lock**
*The Whizzer Series.*—(Over Arm Hook Variations.)

71a—Have a good base, feet well spread, knees slightly bent, and body under control. A swings his left arm high over and in front of B.
71b—A turns and hooks his left arm over B's right arm. (A always swings his arm toward the side on which B has his head.) A grips B's left elbow with his right hand. A now has the same lock which was described and illustrated in Chapter VI for executing a Whizzer hold. (See page 44.)

63

72—A proceeds with the execution of any of those to which B may be open. If B is locked tightly and maintains his base so well that a Whizzer will not work, A should shoot his legs back, drive his left hand down for a Reverse Thigh and Far Elbow hold, as was described in Chapter VI. (See page 32.)

*Power Sit Out*

73a—A grasps B's left wrist with his right hand and slides his left arm inside of B's left arm.

73b—A drives his head backward, places his feet out in front, and keeps his feet well spread to maintain a good base.

73c—After A's buttocks reach the mat, he turns either way, depending on the position of B.

# ESCAPES FROM STANDING

*Standing Switch*

74a—This is an ideal position from which to execute a powerful and effective switch. A reaches over B's right arm (the long arm) with his right arm, and grasps inside of B's right leg with his right hand.

74b—A drives his head backward against B's right shoulder and places his feet out in front. As A's buttocks reach the mat, A starts swinging to B's right, driving his buttocks out and away from B. This should force B's right shoulder to the mat. A completes a reversal by swinging behind B while B's shoulder is held to the mat.

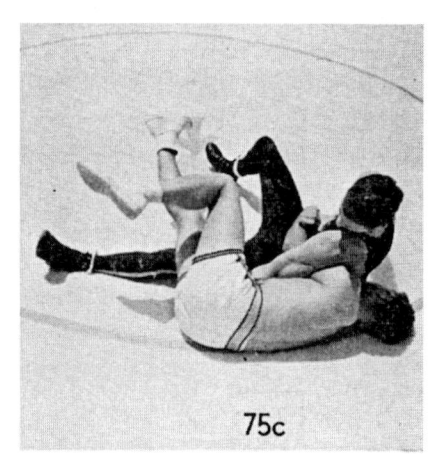

*Combination Switch and Side Roll*

75a—A should set this up by first faking a switch to the right side, then turning to his left. With his right hand A grasps B's right wrist (the long arm).

75b—A steps with his left foot in front of B's right foot and swings his left hand in front of B with the palm of his left hand placed against B's right side.

75c—Simultaneously, A sits down, keeping a straight left leg. As B hits the mat A releases B's right wrist and turns into B for a reversal.

CHAPTER X
# Breakdowns and Rides

Riding and keeping your opponent under control after you have brought him to the mat is one of the most important phases of wrestling. There are a few basic ideas to be observed, but ninety per cent of your ability to Ride effectively will have to come from what you learn and not more than ten per cent from what you are taught.

**RIDING**

*Basically, Riding consists of maintaining your balance and destroying your opponent's balance.* Riding can be defined as the art of securing and maintaining control of your opponent.

The reason that Riding is of such importance, other than for the purpose of garnering "points," is that it is preliminary to securing a fall. If you are unable to Ride him (control your opponent) the possibility of pinning him is indeed remote.

The late Edward Clarke Gallagher of Oklahoma A. and M. College, who is recognized as the Dean of all American wrestling coaches, used the analogy of the underneath wrestler representing a table. The table has four points of support as has the wrestler who is underneath on his hands and knees. If you destroy one of the legs of a table, the direction of least support would be at an angle of 45 degrees in the direction of the leg which has been destroyed. Likewise, in destroying the base of a wrestler, the general idea is to destroy one of his four points of support and drive him at an angle of 45 degrees in that direction. In learning to Ride this principle should always be kept in mind.

Breaking your opponent down, that is, getting him flattened on the mat in a prone position, is your immediate objective after securing a position of advantage. Getting your opponent in this prone position accomplishes the two-fold objective of eliminating most of his possibilities of Escape by destroying his base and making him vulnerable to some Pinning Combination. When you have taken your opponent off balance and have him down in this prone position, you must keep your weight distributed to *maintain your balance*. At the same time, you must *"pump" your weight into him*, wearing him down by making him carry *all* of your weight. Do not make the mistake of using your strength more than is necessary by just trying to hold onto him. You will be more effective and *much more secure* by learning to control your balance, destroy your opponent's base, and distribute your weight in such a manner that your opponent will be at the greatest disadvantage. In learning to Ride, you have an excellent opportunity to learn to relax. All coaches recognize the value and also the difficulty of teaching an athlete how to relax. *This must be learned; it cannot be taught.* A splendid exercise designed to develop this essential quality is to practice Riding by exerting the minimum effort in controlling your opponent while maintaining control over your own balance.

All beginners in wrestling can learn much about Riding by practicing the following drill for a few minutes daily before they attempt to learn any technical holds from this position.

## POINT OF CONTACT DRILL

From the Referee's Position, the top man places his chest on his opponent's back but does not use his arms or legs to secure a wrestling hold. The underneath man attempts to displace the top wrestler by moving, turning, sitting out, twisting, or rolling about the mat, but is not permitted to use any lock, grip, or wrestling hold. It should be the purpose of the top man to expend a minimum amount of effort while maintaining his position of advantage. This exercise is as beneficial to the man underneath as it is to the one on top.

*Break Downs*

These holds are described and illustrated by starting from the Referee's Position.

*Inside Crotch Pry.*—Followed up with a near Bar Lock.
    76a—A drops his right knee behind B's buttocks. With his right hand A lifts on B's inside right thigh. With his left hand he pulls on B's left arm at the bend of B's elbow, driving him forward at an angle of 45 degrees onto B's left shoulder.
    76b—A retains the grip he has on B's left arm, encircles B's waist with his right arm, and drives into him with his right shoulder. (Do not allow yourself to get off balance while you are driving your opponent.)

76c—From this tight riding position, it is "B's next move." When B attempts to re-establish his base by coming to his knees, A secures a single Bar Lock on B's left wrist with his left hand. A now has a Bar Lock and Waist Ride.

76d—A drives his left forearm over B's left upper arm, retains a tight Waist Lock, and keeps B's left shoulder "ground" into the mat. With this hold A is in a position to exert considerable pressure, keep B under control, and "open him up" for a fall

(This same hold may be started by pushing forward by a quick thrust with your left hand against opponent's left elbow.)

*Near Ankle.*—Followed up with a "Two on One" Bar Lock.

77a—A places his right knee behind B's buttocks. With his left hand A grasps B's instep, pulls up, and places it on his left thigh next to his body. A retains a tight Waist Lock with his right arm.

77b—A keeps B's left foot tucked in this position, pulls on B's left arm, and drives B down onto his left shoulder. A keeps his weight distributed to prevent B straightening his leg.

77c—When B attempts to re-establish his base, A secures a "Two on One" Bar Lock by grasping B's left wrist with both hands. A is now in an excellent position to secure a fall with a Bar Lock and Half Nelson.

*Head Lever.*—Followed up with a Chicken Wing.

78a—A slips his left hand from B's left elbow and grasps B's left wrist. A lifts on B's right thigh with an Inside Crotch Pry, drives his head against B's left armpit, and at the same time A pulls outward on B's wrist.

78b—A applies pressure with his head to keep B in this prone position.

78c—A can improve his position by sliding his left arm under B's left forearm and grasping with his left hand on B's upper left arm. This lock is known as a "Chicken Wing" Ride. Several effective Pinning Combinations can be gone into from here.

*Rear Crotch and Far Elbow.*—Followed up with an Inside Crotch and Half Nelson. This is a simple but effective hold which may sometimes be used to secure a fall in quick order.

79a—A reaches under B's left arm and grasps B's right elbow with his left hand.

79b—A grasps B's rear crotch with his right hand, pulls on B's right elbow, and drives B down at an angle of 45 degrees on his right shoulder.

79c—A takes an Inside Crotch hold with his right hand and either a Half Nelson or a Reverse Half Nelson with his left arm for a Pinning Combination (depending on whether B attempts to turn toward or away from A).

*Far Ankle.*—Followed up with an Inside Crotch.

This Ride has been used as a "stalling" Ride more than any other. It is especially conservative, easy to learn, and has the important advantage of controlling an opponent by attacking only his "hind-quarters." Beginning wrestlers are liable to make the mistake of working too high on their opponent. For that reason it is important they learn the effectiveness of controlling an opponent's leg before trying to master the more difficult Rides.

80a—A grasps B's right instep with his right hand, pulls out on B's left knee with his left hand, and pushes with his head against B's left side.

80b—A forces B down onto his right buttocks by pulling in on B's right foot with his right hand and pushing with his head.

80c—A takes an Inside Crotch hold with his left arm and catches deeply around the small of B's back with his right arm. This is a devastating Ride. From here A must be alert to shoot his right arm in for a Half Nelson.

*Four Point Ride.*—Followed up with a Snap Back.

This is also somewhat of a "stalling" Ride. Its principal value is to make your opponent attempt a Sit Out by eliminating other possibilities of escape.

81a—A reaches over B's arm with his corresponding hands. A straddles B's feet with his knees. By riding over B's arms and legs in this manner, A has eliminated most of B's possibilities of escape. B usually considers the most feasible maneuver to be a Sit Out.

# BREAKDOWNS AND RIDES

81b—When B starts a Sit Out, A gives partial resistance by squeezing with his knees and pulling tightly with his hands over B's arms. A slides his right arm over B's right arm and deeply around his back, grasps B's chin with his left hand, and settles down on him with his knees well spread behind.

81c—A now has a Reverse Body Lock and Head Chancery, more commonly known as a "Snap Back." It is an effective pin hold.

*Cross Face and Far Ankle.*—Followed with an Arm Scissors and Reverse Double Wrist Lock.

This is an effective variation of a Cross Face. Fine balance, timing, agility, and practice are required to execute properly this maneuver. This hold is not designed for beginners.

82a—A secures a Far Ankle and Cross Face and drives with his chest against B, causing B to brace with his arms.

82b—A lifts B's right ankle, exerts pressure with a Cross Face, and hooks over B's left arm with his left leg. B is forced over on his right shoulder.

82c—A spins around B's head, hooking B's left arm with his right leg as he spins around.

82d—A secures a Reverse Double Wrist Lock on B's right arm and retains a Scissors on B's left arm to obtain a fall.

### Body Scissors

Learning all the uses, possibilities and variations of the Scissors holds in wrestling is almost an "education" in itself. Many important aspects of this method of attack will be considered. Again, it is called to your attention that the various holds and locks can be put together in any desired combination. This is especially true in using Scissors and further illustrates what is meant by chain wrestling.

The first problem to be considered is how to drive your leg in so you can obtain a grapevine on your opponent's leg. Before this can be done, your opponent's arm must be pushed forward in order that you can drive your corresponding leg in without his being able to reach under your leg and pull you over his head. After an opening has been created by pushing forward on either the near or far arm, the corresponding leg must be snapped in hard and fast from the side.

The Body Scissors has been employed to a large extent for the limited purpose of Riding, but it can also be used as a most effective means of Pinning. If you will pull up with your grapevining leg or legs, "pump" your weight into your opponent, and not permit him to roll with you, it can be used with devastating effect in wearing your opponent down and "softening him up" for a fall.

The final phase of pinning with Body Scissors will be considered in the following chapter.

### Stretcher (Top Body Scissors)

83a—A steps up with his left foot even with B's left ankle and drives his arms under B's corresponding arms.

83b—A drives his right leg in from the side over B's right leg and plants his right foot on the mat in between B's knees. A immediately whips in his left leg from the left side in like manner.

83c—A pulls up with his heels and drives forward with all his weight centered in the small of B's back.

83d—A obtains a Double Bar Lock with A's hands grasping B's corresponding wrists.

83e—A may be able to straighten B's arms out in front of him.

83f—A may pull up on B's head and keep him flattened out by pushing B's head in the opposite direction to which B attempts to turn.

(Keep your knees spread and your ankles locked. You do not get pressure by squeezing with your knees, but by lifting with your heels.)

*Three Quarter Stretcher*

84a—A hops to the rear of B, comes up onto his feet and blocks outward against B's left elbow with his left forearm. A also uses the pressure of his chest to keep B pushed forward. A whips his left foot in and plants it between B's knees.

84b—A hooks with his right foot under B's right instep. A drives his right arm under B's right elbow, lifts up with his left leg and pulls up on B's right elbow simultaneously.

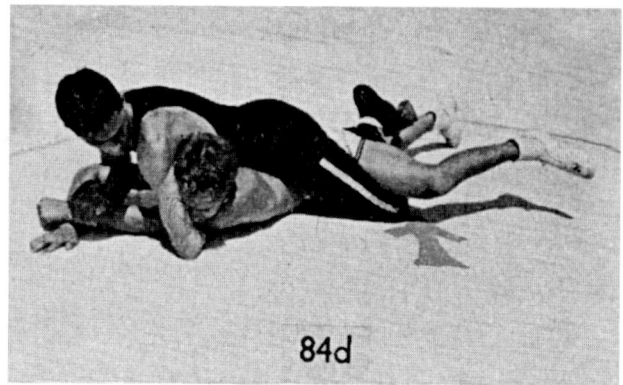

84c—As A drives forward, he brings his left elbow against the right side of B's face, flattening B to the mat. A can cause B considerable discomfort by "pumping" his weight into him. (Again, your knees should be spread to give you a better base. Keep the foot of the leg with which you Grapevine hooked over your other heel.)

84d—A slight variation of this is for A to reach under and across B's face and grasp B's left elbow with his left hand. This lock can cause excruciating punishment.

*Cross Body*

85a—A gets a Grapevine with his left leg in the same manner as has already been suggested, but this time A shoots his foot all the way in and hooks it over the calf of B's left leg. A drives his right hand under B's right elbow, plants his left elbow on B's neck, and grasps his left wrist with his own right hand (a Bar Nelson). If B attempts to stand, A forces down on B's neck with a Bar Nelson.

85b—From here A can hang on and let B make the next move with the hope that B may "hang himself" by falling into a Pinning trap. A prevents B from "drilling" him (driving A's head into the mat) by using a Cross Face with his left arm.

85c—If B "scoops" with his left knee and bridges back into A, A prevents B from Pinning him by kicking B's right foot out from under him.

85d—A may secure a Two On One Bar Lock on either of B's wrists, release his Grapevine and, with his knees on the outside, A keeps his insteps hooked under B's knees. (This is popularly called the "Crab Ride.")

*The Figure Four Scissors.*—This scissors hold is set up in the same manner as has already been described.

> 86a—A shoots his left foot all the way across under B's body, grasps his own left ankle with his right hand, then hooks behind his own right knee with his left foot.
>
> 86b—A keeps his right foot hooked behind the calf of B's right leg. A shoots his body forward in the same manner as was described in the use of the Stretcher.
>
> 86c—A keeps B flattened in a prone position.

CHAPTER XI

# Pinning Combinations

The "ground-work" has now been laid for securing a fall. Getting behind your opponent, riding, and "breaking him down" are all prerequisite to Pinning him. Through the ages, there have been many "Fancy Dan" methods figured out to pin a man, but the simple, direct and basic maneuvers are what "pay off" in a hard match against a worthy opponent.

**INSIDE CROTCH PINNING COMBINATIONS**

In the preceding Chapters there have been many references made to an Inside Crotch hold, and many circumstances suggested wherein this hold could be obtained. We will now consider the technical points to be observed in securing a fall from this position. *Always reach deeply under the buttocks and lift. (To prevent bridging.) Keep your body perpendicular to opponent with your weight centered on your chest.* If opponent is attempting to turn toward you, apply a Half Nelson, a Cross Face, or a Double Arm Tie Up. If he is attempting to turn away from you, apply a Reverse Half Nelson, or a Reverse Cross Face.

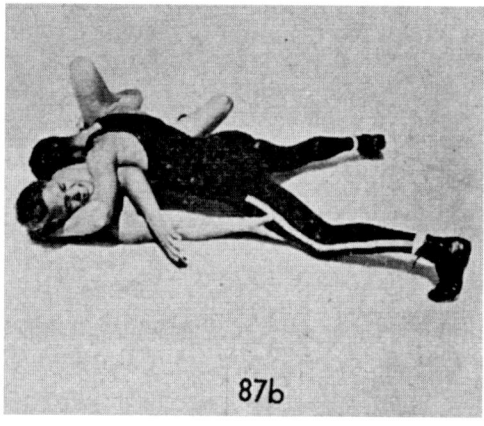

87a—Inside Crotch and Half Nelson.
87b—Inside Crotch and Cross Face.
87c—Inside Crotch and Double Arm Tie Up.

PINNING COMBINATIONS 77

87d—Inside Crotch and Reverse Half Nelson.
87e—Inside Crotch and Reverse Cross Face.

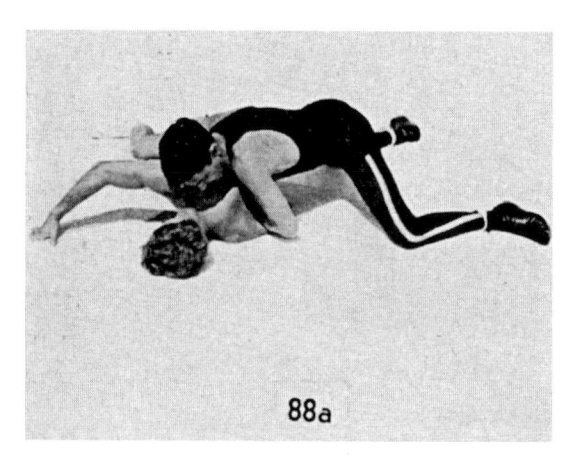

*Bar Lock and Half Nelson*

88a—Preparation for this Pinning Combination can be made when you have opponent broken down with *any* Bar Arm Ride. Keep your weight well distributed and drive into opponent with your chest. The effect of this pressure will increase opponent's desire to re-establish his base by coming back upon his hands and knees.

88b—When B plants his right hand on the mat in his endeavor to establish a base, A pivots on his chest and simultaneously drives across to B's right side. A shoots his right hand through at the crook of B's arm, keeps driving forward, and plants his right hand *on the top of* B's head. *(Maximum leverage is obtained by applying the pressure against B's elbow and the top of his head.)*

88c—After A has driven up on B and forced B's elbow up so that B's right arm is on a line parallel with B's body, A pulls B's head toward him and shoots his arm all the way in for a deep Half Nelson. A's right hand should be "pan-caked" between his chest and opponent's chest, with palm up.

88d—A keeps perpendicular to B with all of his weight on B's chest, pulls up with his right elbow to prevent B from bridging, and retains his grip on B's wrist with his left hand.

**Bar Lock and Figure Four Head Scissors**
　　This most effective pin hold can be set up in precisely the same manner as the preceding hold.

　　　　89a—A catches under B's right elbow, preparatory to stepping across to B's right side.

　　　　89b—A keeps his weight on B so that B will be held down on his left shoulder.

PINNING COMBINATIONS 79

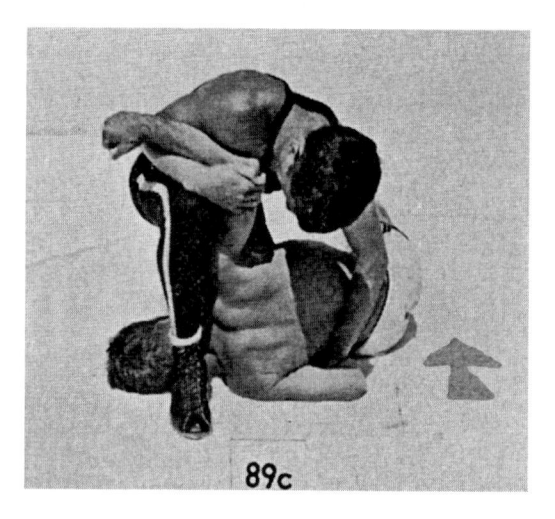

89c—A plants the heel of his right foot behind B's head.

89d—A lunges forward, slides his right leg well under B's neck, and engages his right foot behind his left knee for a Figure Four Head Scissors. A keeps B's right arm extended by grasping B's right wrist, pulls up on B's neck with his right knee, and keeps the thigh of his left leg pressed against B's chest.

***Bar Lock and Farther Under Arm Hook***

This lock makes an effective Ride, but its greatest value lies in the many Pinning Combinations that can be worked from it. Several such Pinning Combinations from this position will be illustrated and described.

90—To obtain this lock, A first secures a near Bar Lock on B's left arm. With his right hand, A reaches under B's right arm close to B's elbow, pulls it tightly to B's body with his right elbow pressed into the small of B's back. A keeps the pressure on B with his weight well distributed and goes into one of the following four pin holds.

*Reverse Body Lock*

91a—If B rolls to his left, A releases his Bar Lock with his left hand and pulls B toward him with his right hand.

91b—A drives his left elbow under B's left armpit. A retains the lock on B's right elbow with his right hand slides his legs out behind and, when B starts to bridge, A slips his left arm well under B's back. A keeps his weight centered on B's chest.

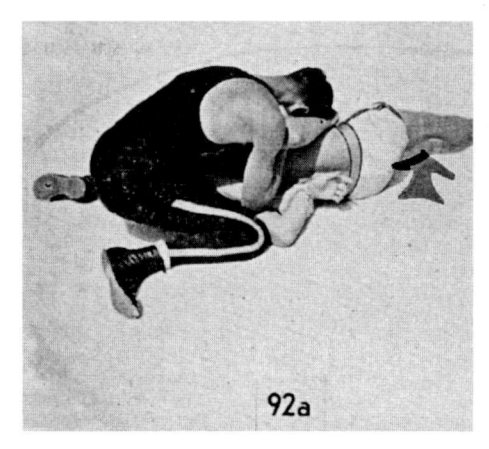

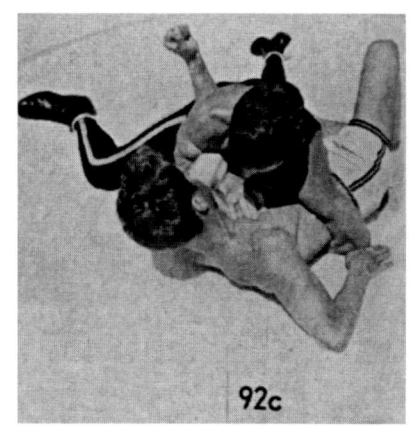

*Arm Bar and Body Lock*

92a—A drives around to his left until B's head comes between A's knees.

92b—A releases B's left wrist and drives his left arm through under B's right elbow.

92c—A releases with his right hand and secures a fall with an Arm Bar and Body Lock.

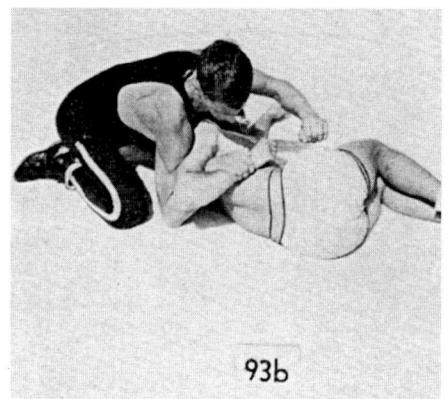

*Key Lock*

93a—A drives his left knee against the left side of B's head and pulls up on B's right elbow with his right hand.

93b—A releases B's left wrist, swings his left arm over B's right forearm, and catches B's right shoulder with his left hand. A catches over his own left upper arm with his right hand to complete a Key Lock.

93c—To make this more secure, A keeps his base on his left leg with his buttocks against B's head. A squeezes with his left arm and pulls up with his right arm to exert pressure.

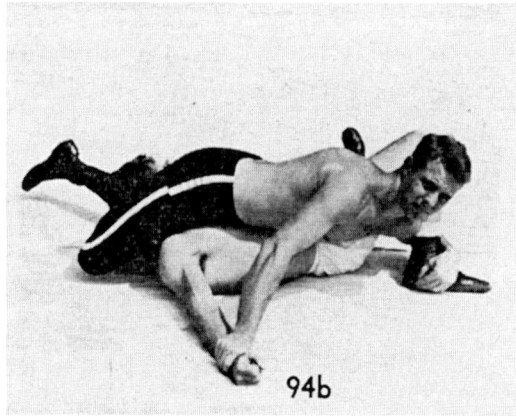

*Figure Four Head Scissors*

This hold is most effective and can be used in a great variety of situations. A Bar Lock and Farther Underarm Hook Ride is an ideal position from which to obtain it.

94a—A slides his right leg under B's neck and whips his left leg over B's head to obtain a Head Scissors.

94b—A rotates his body toward B and secures B's head in the crook of A's right leg. A locks the instep of his right foot behind the hock of his own left knee. A centers his weight on B's chest and hooks under the instep of B's right foot with his left arm when B undertakes to bridge.

## Arm Lock and Body Press

95a—From a Head Lever Ride (see page 69), A encircles B's waist with his right arm and clasps B's left upper arm with his right hand.

95b—A drives into B and swings to B's right side.

95c—A retains his hold, drives his shoulder into B's chest and forces B's shoulders to the mat.

## Modified Three Quarter Nelson

This hold is appropriate when opponent permits his head to rest on the mat.

96a—A plants his right foot in between B's feet, scoops toward him, hooking B's left leg under his own right leg

96b—A places his left hand on B's head and pulls down. With his right hand A reaches under B's left arm and secures a wrestler's grip with his hands locked over B's head.

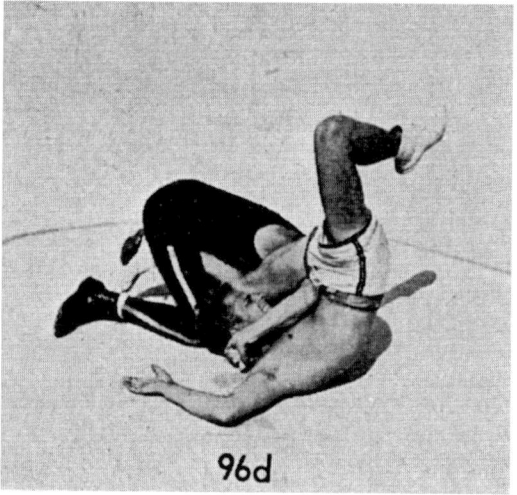

96c—A keeps B's head pulled to the mat and slides around to his left, forcing B over onto his shoulders. A should not permit his left hip to sag to the mat.
96d—A keeps on his knees in order to maintain his base and prevents B somersaulting.

### Double Bar Arm Lock

97a—From a single Bar Lock Ride, A reaches over B's right arm with his right hand.
97b—A hooks over B's arm at the elbow and drives his right arm all the way through behind B's back.
97c—A releases his Bar Lock grasp, drives his left arm through under B's neck and locks his hands in a wrestler's grip over B's left arm pit. A shoots his legs back, keeps his chin pressed against B's right shoulder, and maintains a tight grip for a fall.

### Chicken Wing (The Bar Hammerlock)

From this Ride one may maneuver, into the following Pinning Combinations.

*Reverse Body Lock*

98a—A pulls upward on B's left shoulder with his left arm, drives hard, forcing B over on his right shoulder.

98b A spins around B's head forcing B over onto his back. A keeps B's left arm locked under his left chest, slides his right arm deeply under B's back, keeps his weight distributed, and secures a fall.

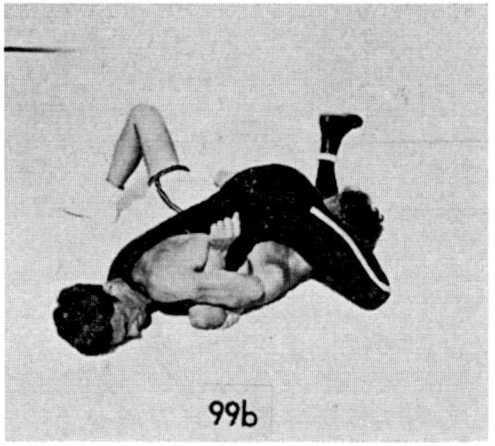

*Step Over Head Scissors*

99a—A plants his left foot to the right of B's head, keeping B's left arm barred.

99b—A lunges forward, sliding his left leg under B's neck and secures a Figure Four Head Scissors. A locks B's left arm and lifts B's head with his Scissors Hold to secure a fall.

PINNING COMBINATIONS 85

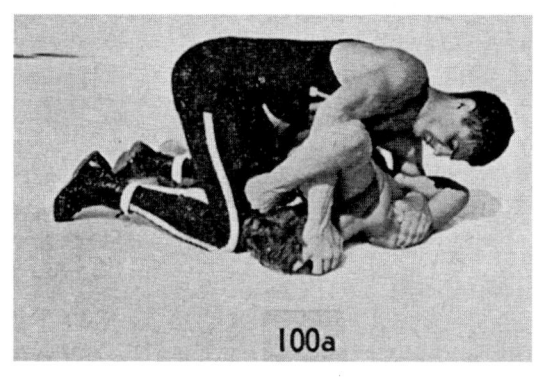

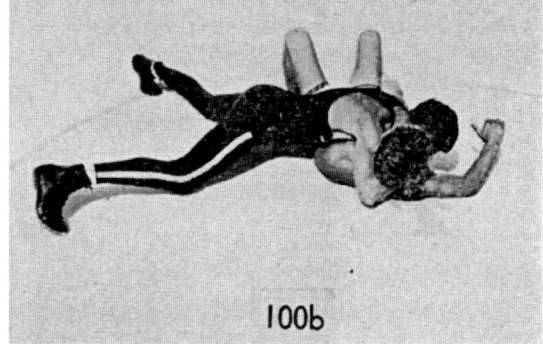

*Chicken Wing and Half Nelson*

100a—If B rolls toward A, A pivots over to B's right side and secures a Half Nelson with his right arm.

100b—If B slips his left arm out of A's Chicken Wing, A grabs B's left wrist and pins B with a wrist grasp and Half Nelson. (If A is unable to grasp B's left wrist, A may get an Inside Crotch hold with his left arm and pin B with an Inside Crotch and Half Nelson or an Inside Crotch and Reverse Half Nelson.)

**Body Scissors**

Riding with the Scissors has already been discussed in the preceding chapter. The methods of converting these Rides into Pinning Combinations will now be described and illustrated.

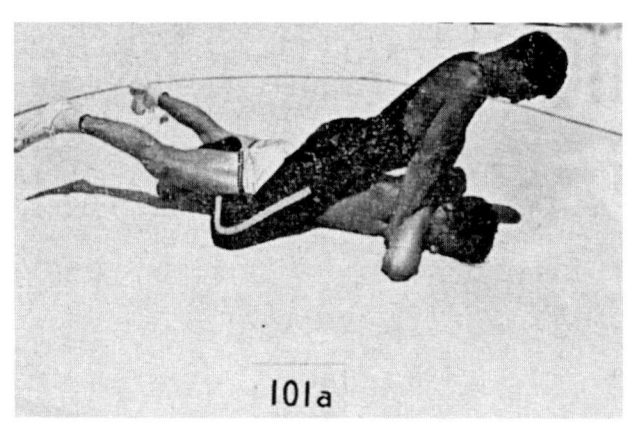

*Stretcher.*—Converted into a Front Body Scissors.

101a—After A has flattened B out with a Stretcher Ride, A secures a Double Bar Lock. From this point, B will determine, by his actions, whether A should apply a Half Nelson with his right or left hand.

101b—If B turns to his left, A lifts with his right hand under B's right elbow, plants his right hand on the top of B's head for the start of a Half Nelson. By driving into B, it is possible for A to exert considerable pressure on B at this juncture, so A should not be in a hurry to turn B over.

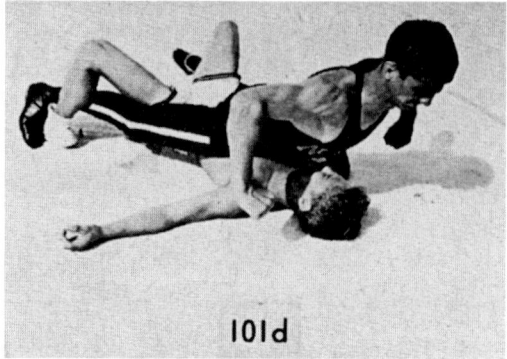

101c—A unhooks his ankles, gives a quick pull on B's head and shoots his arm in deeply around B's neck for a deep Half Nelson. A drives forward and at the same time hooks his own ankles under B's thighs in a Front Body Scissors. A keeps his knees spread, pulls up on B's head with the Half Nelson to prevent B from bridging.

101d—When B attempts to bridge, A may release his ankle lock and take a Double Grapevine by locking his feet inside of B's ankles.

*Double Bar Nelson*

102a—From a Stretcher Ride, A locks under both of B's arms with his corresponding hands and extends B's arms forward in front of B's head. A lifts on B's right elbow and drives his right hand through for a Half Nelson. A holds on with his left hand under B's left elbow until his right hand comes through in applying the Half Nelson.

102b—With his right hand A grasps B's upper left arm. A now has a Double Bar Nelson. A obtains an easy fall by falling over on his left side and keeping B's arms drawn together. A has such a marked superiority on leverage with this hold that he must be extremely cautious of injuring B.

# PINNING COMBINATIONS

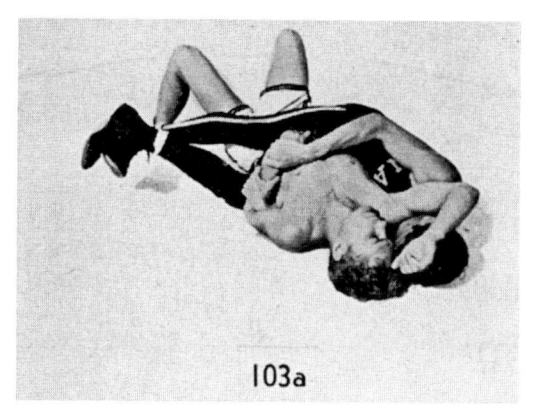

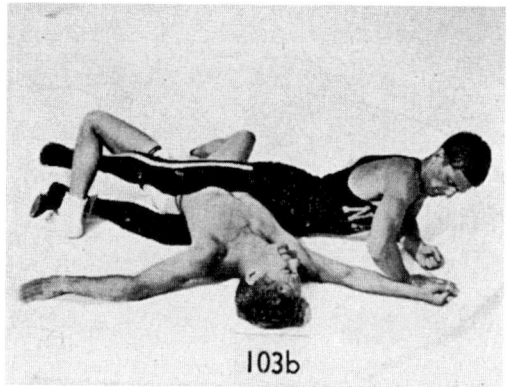

*Knee Lock*

103a—A takes a Two on One Bar Lock on B's left wrist and a loose Body Scissors. A permits B to roll to his left. A keeps his legs around B in a flat Body Scissors and retains his Two on One Bar Lock.

103b—When B attempts to bridge, A locks with the insteps of both of his feet behind B's lower left leg. A may now turn loose with his hands and hold B securely with the Knee Lock.

*Figure Four Body Scissors*

104a—A flattens B prone on the mat by using the same methods as were employed in the Stretcher.

104b—With his left leg hooked around B's body, A takes a Half Nelson with his right hand and "cuts down" on B with his Scissors.

104c—A drives forward, forcing B's shoulders to the mat. A keeps his chest low so B cannot get his right arm free and keeps his right foot hooked over the calf of B's right leg. (The effectiveness of this hold lies in its punishing qualities. Most exponents of this Scissors hold use it to "torture" their opponent into submission rather than relying on the simple mechanics of it. The way it is commonly used borders onto the illegal.)

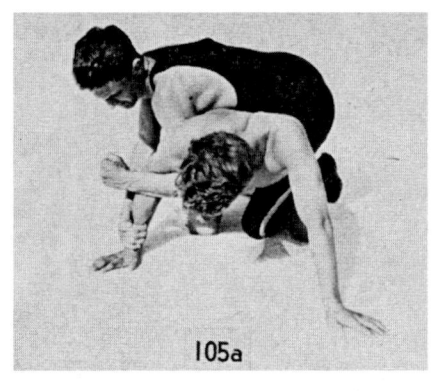

*Guillotine.*—(Fall from a Cross Body Scissors)

There are several methods of obtaining this effective Pin hold. One of the most direct methods is:

> 105a—From a Cross Body Ride with a Grapevine on B's left leg, A grasps B's right wrist with his right hand and pulls it toward him. A reaches behind and under B's right arm with his left arm.
>
> 105b—With both of his arms A pulls B's right arm upward over his head and secures B's right arm behind his own back.
>
> 105c—A pulls backward, settling on his left buttock, and takes a Figure Four Scissors on B's left leg. A grabs B's head with both of his hands, pulls B's head toward him and "cuts down" with his left leg, forcing B's shoulders to the mat.

*Leg Split*

This is another hold that borders onto the illegal. The methods described and illustrated here are also effective for obtaining a Guillotine.

> 106a—From a Cross Body Ride with a Grapevine on B's left leg, A grabs the instep of B's foot with his right hand and catches inside of B's right thigh with his left hand.
>
> 106b—A pulls upward on B's right leg, settles down on his left buttock, and secures a Figure Four Scissors on B's left leg.
>
> 106c—A may Grapevine with his left leg and push with his right foot against B's left heel.

# PINNING COMBINATIONS

106d—A may grab B's right wrist and lock B's right arm in an extended position behind B's right leg. A supplies pressure and rocks B back on his shoulders for a fall.

106e—Instead of grabbing B's wrist, A may obtain a Guillotine by driving his left elbow under B's right arm.

106f—A pulls B's head toward him and may continue in the same manner as has already been described in the preceding hold for securing a fall.

## *Counters for Pin Holds*

In reality, all Escapes from the underneath position on the mat can be classified as Counters for Pin Holds. Escapes will be thoroughly considered in Chapter XII. The greatest single factor in preventing your opponent from getting a fall is to move before he does and not let him "get set" on you to apply a Pinning hold. In a large percentage of cases an inexperienced man will do more toward Pinning himself than his opponent will toward securing a fall.

*The worst position in wrestling is on your back; the next worse is to be flattened out in a prone position.* Do not attempt to initiate an escape when you are flattened out on your stomach because you have no base. Against an experienced wrestler you will be permitted to turn, *but he will not turn with you;* when you have turned onto your back he will clamp down on you with some Pin hold. From a prone position, endeavor to get back to your hands and knees *by pulling your knees up under you.* Do not try to push back up with your arms.

*When on Back*

107a—A keeps his body parallel with B's, pushes with his under hand against B's thigh, bridges on his head and shoulder, and *drives his other hand between B's chest and his own chest.*

107b—*A should not grab B's head, nor try to roll toward B with his arm pushing against B's shoulder;* the mechanical leverage would be against A.

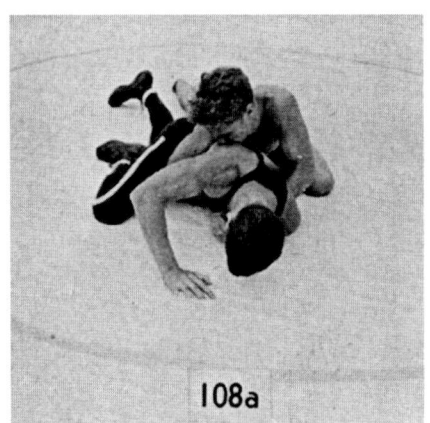

*When on Stomach.*—(Opponent has a Bar Lock)

108a—A draws his right knee up under his body.

108b—A then pulls his left knee up under him.

108c—To break the Bar Lock, A straightens his arm and twists against B's thumb. From this position, A continues with an Escape before B has an opportunity to get him off balance again.

PINNING COMBINATIONS

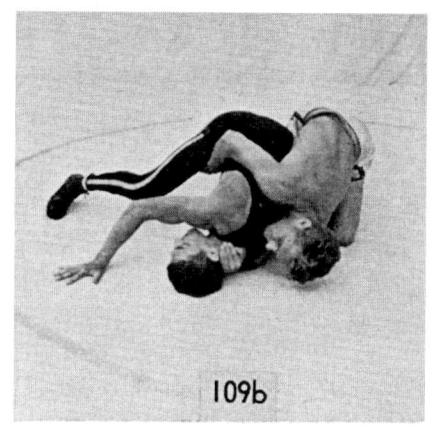

*To Block a Half Nelson*

109a—Assume B is attempting to obtain a Half Nelson from A's left side. A pulls down with his left shoulder, lifts with his head, then "looks away (turns his head away from B). A comes to his right foot for additional support and to protect his base. A reaches with his left hand over B's fingers and pulls B's hand off his neck.

109b—If B attempts to obtain a Half Nelson without first breaking A down, A may use a Near Wing Lock. A hooks above B's left elbow with the crook of his left arm.

109c—A pulls down on his left shoulder, jumps to his left across B's body and places himself in an excellent position to pin B with an Inside Crotch and Half Nelson.

CHAPTER XII

# Escapes from Underneath

Escaping from underneath is one of the most interesting departments of wrestling and is a true test of wrestling ability. Becoming expert in Escapes requires the development of a keen sense of balance, fine co-ordination, perfect timing, and an ability to recognize the situation when a particular move, a hold or combination of holds, will effect an Escape. This phase of wrestling resolves itself into a contest of balance. Every Escape is set up by some maneuver which is designed to draw your opponent off balance in order to facilitate your movement. It is important to learn to go from one hold to another in quick succession to take advantage of an opportunity which arises because your opponent was forced to block preceding maneuvers. Many wrestlers have become highly proficient in grouping their holds with the purpose of making one hold set up another. These holds will be grouped to show how one move can create a situation which will open up a series of related possibilities.

*Stance*

110—Adopting and maintaining a good base in the underneath position is essential. A should have his knees well spread, with most of his weight resting on his knees and feet. A's center of gravity should be at his buttocks. A should keep his head up.

*The Tripod Position*

The following series of Escapes represent a group of holds which can all be set up by making the same initial maneuver. The movement that your opponent makes will largely determine which Escape you will use.

111—A pivots on his left knee, makes a half turn in toward B, places both of his hands on the mat in front of himself, and plants his right foot on the mat out in front of B on a line parallel to B's body. *A's left hand, left knee and right foot should form a right triangle.* A keeps pressure against B by bracing his right foot and driving his left knee in between B's knees. A maintains a strong base in this position by keeping his center of gravity located at his buttocks.

*The Stand Up*

112a—From a Tripod position A grasps over B's fingers with his right hand, "blasts" back into B, and *carries his left elbow high and backward.* This will momentarily drive B backward. A peels B's right hand off from around his waist as he starts to stand.

112b—When A has both of his feet under him, he turns to his left.

112c—If B stands up too, A prevents B from locking his hands around A's waist by grasping B's left hand with his own left hand. A keeps his arms low to prevent B from following up and tackling his legs again.

*The Side Roll*

113a—If B attempts to drop in behind A's legs, or pushes A forward, A grasps B's right wrist with his right hand.

113b—A drives his right knee under B, sits through on his right buttock and rolls B over onto his back. If A has difficulty rolling B, A brings his left foot up inside of B's crotch and Elevates B over.

113c—A drives his feet out perpendicular to B at the instant he rolls B, and turns toward B's legs.

113d—A gets an Inside Crotch hold with his right arm.

113e—A may execute the Side Roll in the same manner by hooking with the crook of his right arm about B's right elbow (instead of grasping B's wrist with his hand) and continuing a roll in the same described manner.

## ESCAPES FROM UNDERNEATH

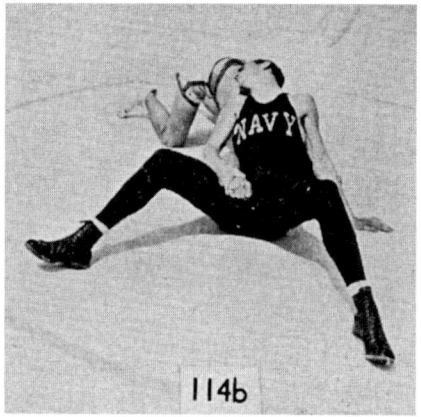

*Sit Out and Turn Out*

If B attempts to get A off balance by pulling A toward him, B will weaken his position for stopping a Sit Out.

114a—A grasps B's right wrist with his right hand, slides his left leg out in front, and drives his head back against B's *right* shoulder.

114b—A keeps his buttocks on the mat as he arches back into B. A retains a tight pull on B's right wrist until B's chest comes in contact with the mat.

114c—A bridges and turns to his right to go behind B.

*Sit Out and Turn In*

The mechanics of this hold are precisely the same as the preceding one, except this time A turns in to A's left instead of out to A's right.

115a—Suppose B has over-hooked A's left arm so that in driving his head back A gets his head on B's left shoulder, or that B is resisting so hard that A cannot turn to his right.

115b—*A drops on his left elbow*, peels B's right hand from around A's waist and turns to his left.

115c—A faces B in neutral position.

*Power Switch*

A most powerful switch can be worked from the Tripod position. It works better if opponent is pulling back.

>116a—When B resists A's turn to the inside, A pivots on his left hand and right foot and drives his right elbow over B's right upper arm.
>
>116b—As A's elbow comes to the mat, A follows up, going behind before B has time to regain a strong base.

*The Whizzer Series*

The mechanics of these holds described in Chapter VI as Take Downs and in Chapter IX as Escapes from Standing can again be employed here, and set up by first assuming a Tripod position.

>117a—A swings his left arm over B's head and hooks over B's right arm. (Good base and hard driving are required to do this.)
>
>117b—A catches B's left elbow preparatory to rolling B to A's right.

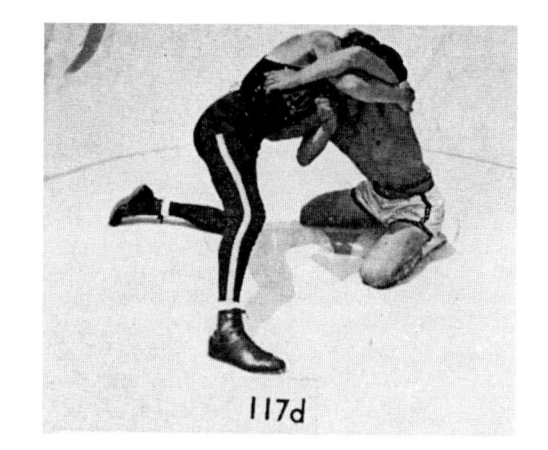

117c—If B is driving forward, A uses a Reverse Thigh and Far Elbow Lock.
117d—If B resists that too strenuously, A uses a Lateral Drop to the opposite side.

*Switch*

In its simplest aspect a Switch is an arm lever obtained by swinging one of your arms over opponent's corresponding arm and catching inside his thigh or under his body with the same hand. By shooting your buttocks away from opponent, tremendous leverage can be applied on opponent's shoulder which will force his chest to come to the mat and give you an opportunity to swing behind him for a reversal. However, a Switch is easy to counter if you know that it is coming. Therefore, it is necessary to draw an opponent out of position by setting it up in some manner. Also, a Switch is a valuable maneuver to set up other avenues of escape, particularly a Sit Out, or to use in combination with other holds.

*The Short Switch*

118a—A plants his left hand on the mat in front of his right shoulder.

118b—A drives off of his right foot, sits through, and lands with his buttocks on the mat even with his left hand. A reaches over B's right arm at the same time that he starts driving forward and catches inside of B's right thigh with his right hand.

118c—A drives his buttocks away from B and turns into him to complete the reversal.

*The Leg Switch*

119a—A moves his left hand forward and plants it on the mat in front of his head. A reaches under his own left arm with his right hand and grasps B's left wrist, trapping B's left hand on the mat.

119b—A swings his left arm over B's left arm and catches under his own left knee with his left hand. A hooks the instep of his left foot inside of B's left thigh.

119c—A lifts, rocks backward, slides his buttocks away from B to obtain greater leverage and turns into B for a reversal.

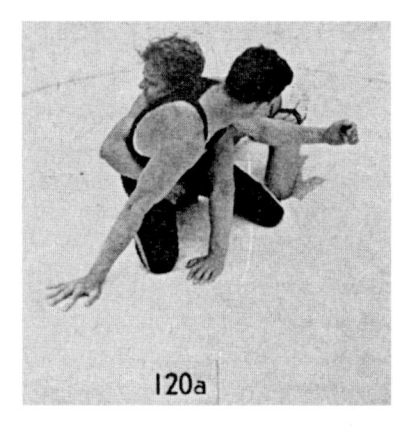

*The Camel Walk Switch*

120a—A starts moving forward on his hands and knees, with an exaggerated swinging motion.

120b—In resisting A's forward movement, B is liable to open himself up on one side or the other for either an outside or inside (leg) Switch.

120c—A executes a Switch on the side to which B has become vulnerable.

*The Combination Switch and Side Roll*

This most powerful Switch has already been described and illustrated in Chapter IX (see page 65). It can again be used here by first coming to your feet.

### The Double Wrist Lock

This hold can be used from any position, viz.; Standing, Underneath or On Top. It can also be used on the Near or Far Side. However, it is employed as a means of escaping from underneath to a greater extent than from any other position.

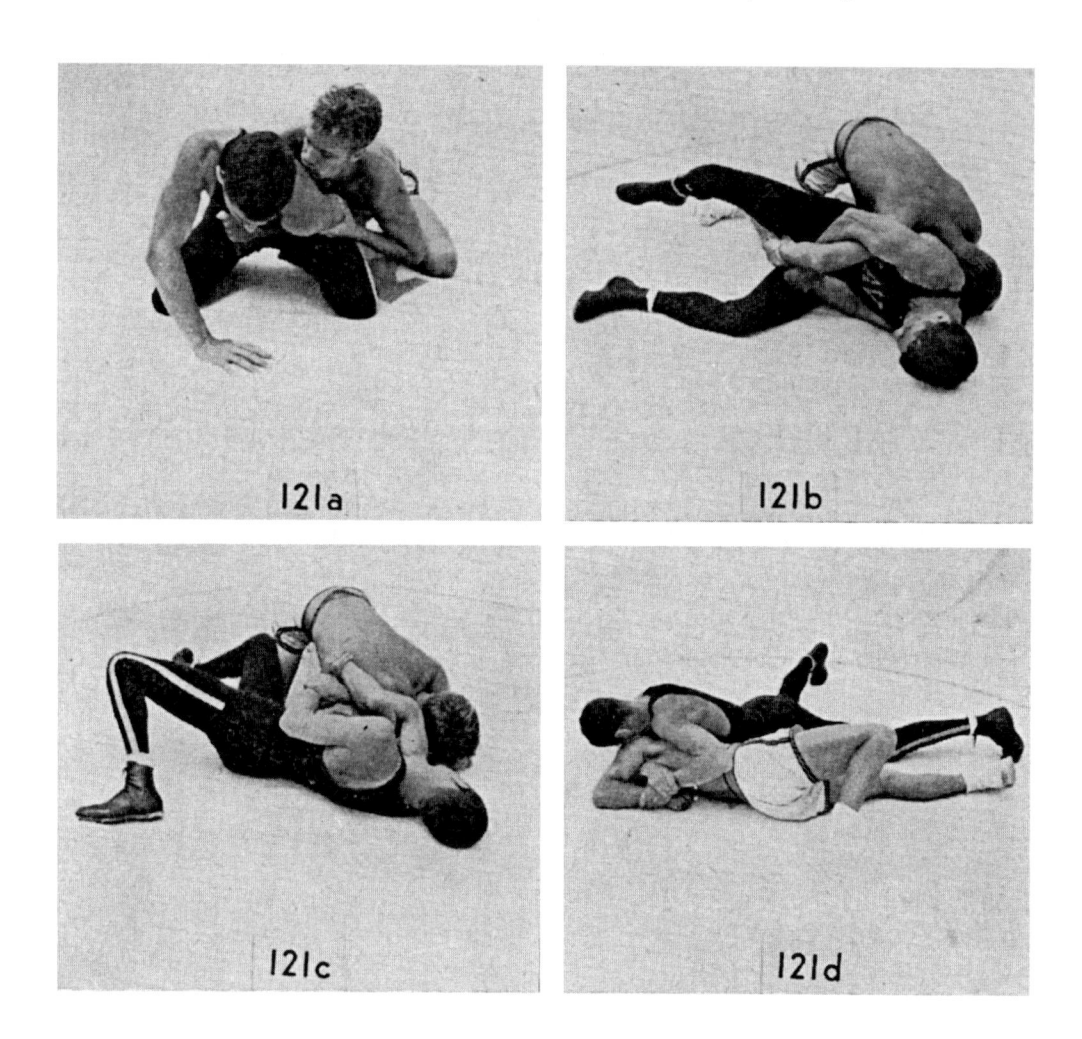

*Outside Double Wrist Lock*

    121a—A moves his right hand forward, plants it on the mat in front of his head, and grasps B's right wrist with his left hand.

    121b—A pushes B's hand to the right as he drops to his left buttock. He keeps his right leg high to block B from swinging across his body to counter the Double Wrist Lock. A reaches his right arm over B's right arm and grabs his own left wrist.

    121c—A slides his buttocks away from B, plants his left foot on the mat, bridges back onto his head, jerks hard with the Double Wrist Lock, and drives toward B forcing B onto his back.

    121d—A retains the Double Wrist Lock to secure a fall, or slips in to a Key Lock in the manner explained in the preceding Chapter (see page 81).

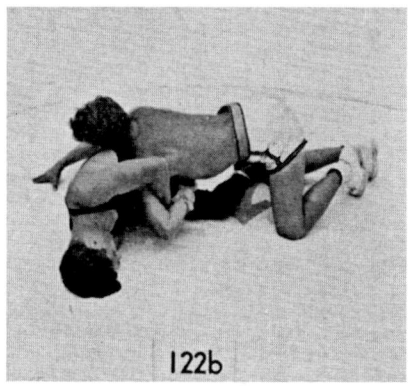

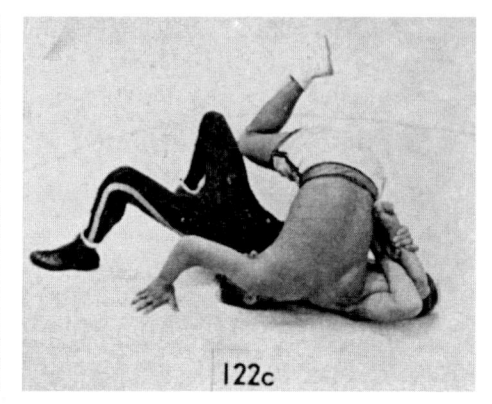

*Inside Double Wrist Lock*

122a—A moves his left hand forward and plants it on the mat in front of his head. A reaches under his own left arm and grasps B's left wrist with his right hand.

122b—A swings toward B, dropping to his right buttock, and obtains a Double Wrist Lock on B's left arm.

122c—A keeps turning in toward B's legs and tries to get his legs out in front of B in a line parallel to B's body. A jerks hard with his Double Wrist Lock, carries B over his left shoulder, *and drives at an angle of 45 degrees to B's body.* (Do not try to force opponent's arm upward over his back; you get much more leverage by using the "45 degree" method.)

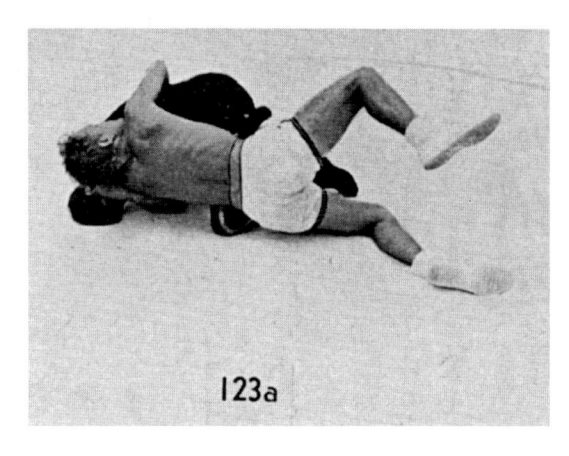

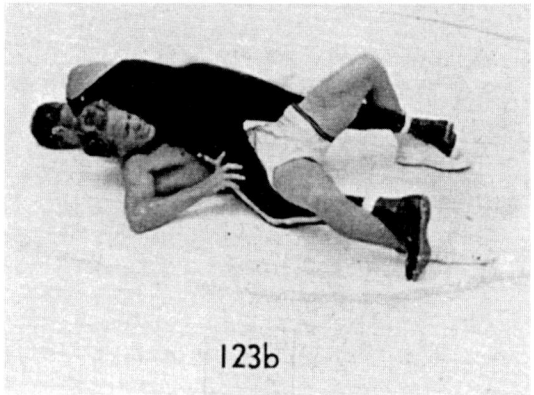

*Wing from Double Wrist Lock*

123a—When A is applying a Double Wrist Lock on B's left arm, if B resists by driving into A, B may weaken his base and be vulnerable to a wing lock on his left side. A pulls downward with his left arm in a forward motion, raises his buttocks high, and steps across B's body with his left leg.

123b—A may apply a Double Grapevine, a Front Body Scissors, or swing around to his left perpendicular to B.

124a

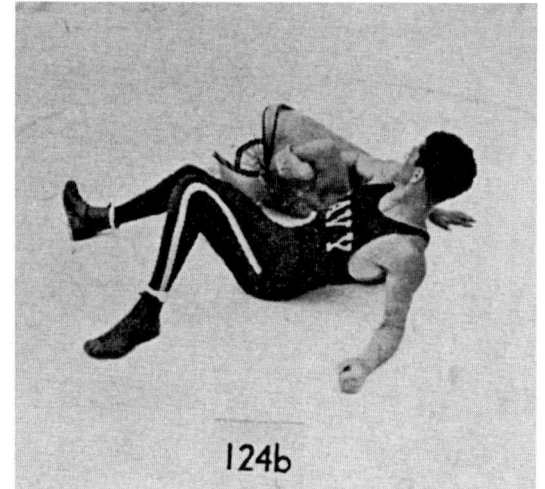

124b

*Double Wrist Lock Slide Out*

124a—This maneuver is a hybrid Double Wrist Lock and Switch. A applies a Double Wrist Lock on B's right arm and hooks B's right leg with his own right leg.

124b—A releases B's right wrist with his left hand and grasps it with his right hand. A maintains this lock on B's wrist, slides his buttocks away from B, to A's left, drops B's right shoulder onto the mat, and pulls in behind B for a reversal.

## The Sit Out

The initial phase of this method of Escape is to shoot your legs out in front of you, keep your legs well spread to maintain a good base and drop your inside elbow to the mat. As you start driving your legs out in front, drive your head backward. It is important that you rest your head against one of your opponent's shoulders. That shoulder represents the fulcrum on which you gain support from which to operate. Your opponent's movements will largely determine which maneuver to use. The simple maneuver of sitting out, driving your head back and turning one way or the other is an excellent warm up exercise and at the same time develops the "feel" of knowing where your opponent is. When it is used as a warm up drill, your opponent should use only passive or semi-resistance. The preliminary move in setting up the situation, which will provide an opportunity for executing the next three holds, is for A to drive his head backward and propel his feet out in front. A must keep his feet spread, with his buttocks on the mat and maintain a good base while in this sitting position.

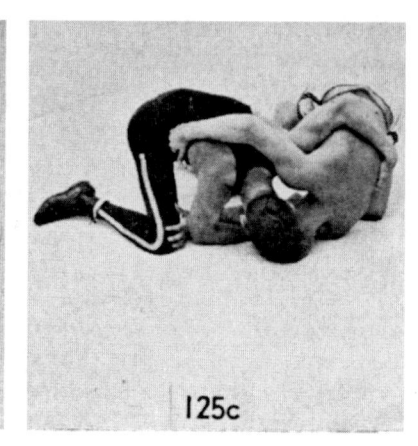

*Craw Fish*

125a—The effect of this initial Sit Out maneuver may result in B being drawn up high on A.

125b—A grasps B's left elbow with his right hand and comes back upon his left foot.

125c—A swings his left arm over B's back, pulls B under him and secures a fall with an Arm Bar and Body Lock.

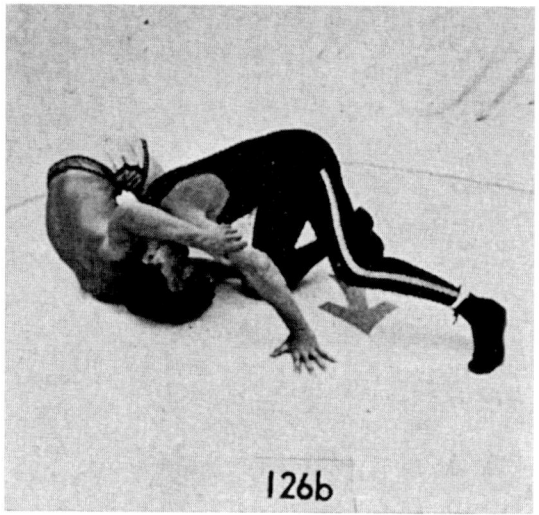

*Head Pull*

126a—If B exposes his head over A's right shoulder, A grasps behind B's head with his right hand.

126b—A swings his buttocks to the left and pulls B under him. (It is usually easier to pull an opponent to the same side on which his head rests.)

# ESCAPES FROM UNDERNEATH

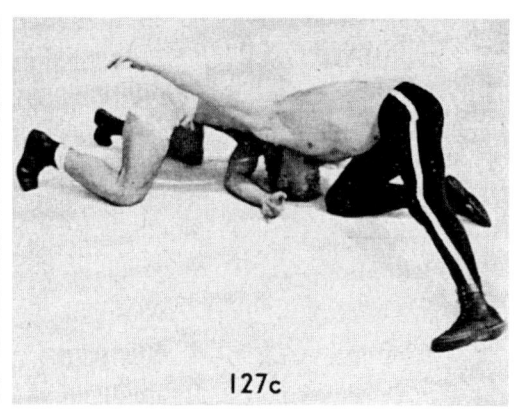

*Fake Switch Sit Out*

127a—A swings through with his left leg and drives his right arm down against B's right arm to simulate a switching maneuver.

127b—A arches back with his head, pulls his left arm in close to his body, and slides forward.

127c—A pivots on his own left shoulder. As A comes to his knees he should be alert to grab B's left arm and pull B onto his back for a possible pin hold.

*The Forward Roll*

This Escape is appropriate when B is working high or is attempting to pull A off balance, especially from the Referee's Position. A may also set it up by leaning forward to entice B to come up high on him.

128a—A drops his head and left shoulder far back under himself and somersaults over B's right arm.

128b—A twists his body as he goes forward in order to land on his knees and face B in a neutral position. (This maneuver can be blocked if B rides back on A's buttocks.)

### The Power Craw Fish

129a—When B is riding A's legs or keeping himself directly to A's rear, A settles back into B on his left buttock.

129b—A reaches his right arm under B's right arm, pulls upward on B's arm and straightens his right leg as he comes back to his knees.

129c—A swings his buttocks away from B ("tails out") as A pulls B over his right shoulder and catches B's right knee with his left hand.

### Elevators

The following series represents a clever and effective group of Escapes involving the use of your legs to lift (elevate) your opponent. The effect of this is to shift your opponent out of position and thus facilitate the use of a hold. This series is not designed for beginners, inasmuch as you may get pinned unless you have developed a fine sense of balance and practiced hours against "sparring partners" until you know exactly what you are doing. Being able to use your legs in all positions is a valuable asset in wrestling. It gives you two more valuable weapons with which to fight.

### Drag and Elevate

130a—A rolls under B, settling on his right thigh and right elbow. A brings his left foot upward into A's crotch and hooks with his left instep inside of B's left thigh.

130b—A catches his left arm under B's left arm and grabs B's left wrist with his right hand. With his left instep against the inside of B's left thigh, A rocks back on his buttocks.

130c—A Elevates with his left leg and carries B to his left, coming behind him for a reversal.

*Drag and Pull Around*

131a—If B attempts to flatten out, A hooks inside of B's right leg with the instep of his left foot. A keeps his right leg outside of B's left leg to aid in preventing B from stepping across A's body.

131b—A drives B's left wrist down between A's thighs, releases with his right hand and grasps B's left leg close to his knee. A pulls on B's left arm and left leg to pull in behind B.

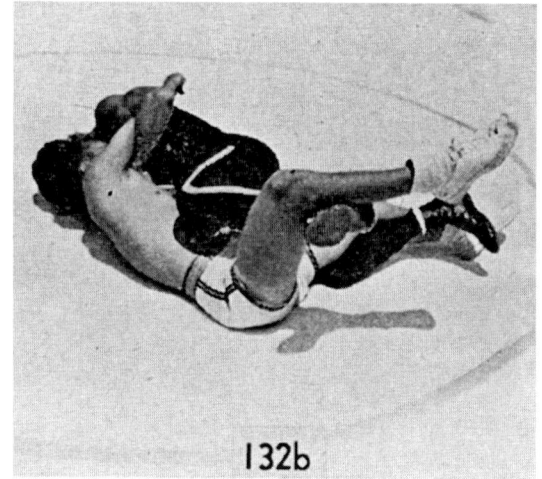

*Reverse Elevator*

132a—If B attempts to step across, A hooks with the instep of his left foot inside of B's right thigh, with his left knee on the right side of B.

132b—A pulls forward on B's left arm, blocks B's left leg from the outside with his right foot, and Elevates B with his left leg, bringing B over onto his back.

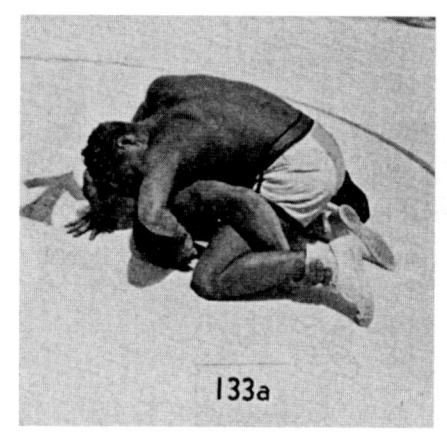

*Pulling Leg Over Head*

133a—With his left hand, A reaches over B's left leg and grasps inside B's left ankle.

133b—A locks B's knee by pulling upward and outward. At the same time A hooks inside of B's right leg with his left leg.

133c—A Elevates with his left knee, pulls with his left arm, and forces B forward over his head. (A must recover quickly before B pivots on his right knee and comes in behind A again.)

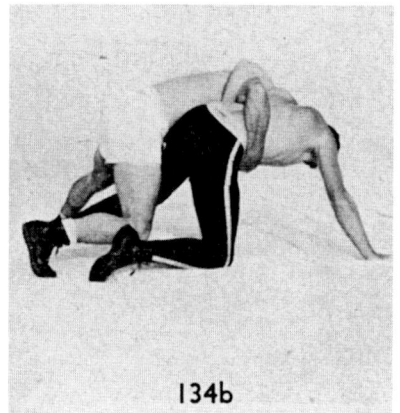

*Over Arm Hook and Slide Out*

134a—With his left arm A overhooks B's right arm. A hooks the instep of his left foot against the thigh of B's right leg.

134b—A rotates toward B and pulls forward and downward on B's left shoulder as A slides his right leg out to get onto his knees.

134c—If B undertakes to maintain his position of advantage by swinging behind A, then A lifts with his left leg, pulls down with his left arm and puts B onto his back for a reversal.

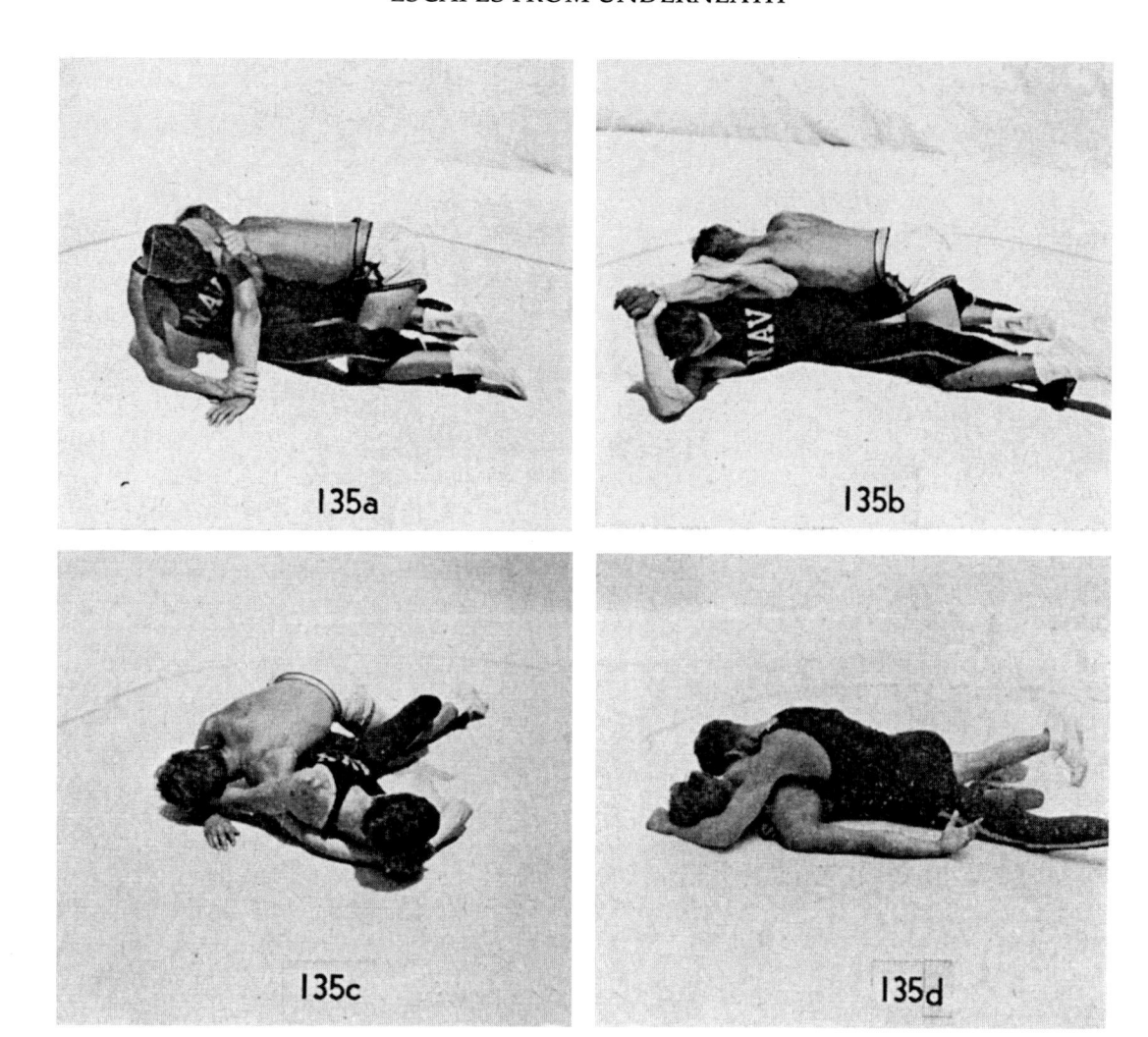

*Arm Pull with Double Grapevine*

135a—A secures a Double Grapevine by hooking from the inside with his left foot and from the outside with his right foot.

135b—A stretches both legs as he pulls B's arm over his head,

135c—A retains a firm grip on B's left wrist and takes a Cross Face with his left arm.

135d—A releases B's left hand and turns into B to complete a reversal.

*The Step Over*

136a—A comes onto his hands and feet in an "all fours" position and starts pulling away from B with his buttocks.

136b—When B resists by pulling with his right arm, A whips his left leg up over B's back, locking his left foot under B's left thigh. A flattens B down to the mat with a Stretcher. (This escape can be blocked by keeping your buttocks raised higher than the opponent's.)

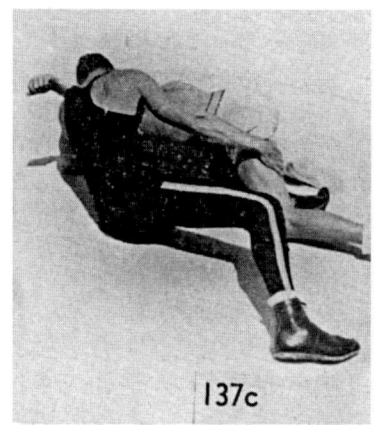

*Slipping a Near Half Nelson*

137a—A catches under B's left upper arm with his left hand, sits through to his left, and pulls B over his left shoulder.

137b—A then slides out to his left and comes behind B for a reversal.

137c—A blocks with his right hand to prevent B from stepping across him. (This hold also works well when B attempts to secure a Far Half Nelson.)

CHAPTER XIII

# Escapes from Special Rides

Consideration must be given to special Rides and a particular method or methods of Escape from such Rides should be understood and practiced. For each Ride there is usually one particular method or methods of Escape which is more feasible than resorting to a general plan of operation.

*Escapes from Cross Body Ride*
  *Method One*
    138—A grasps B's left elbow with his right hand, pulls down, slides his left arm in between B's body and his own. From this position, A slips his hand over B's back.

  *Method Two*
    139a—A drills B's head into the mat by executing a forward roll. When B's head hits the mat, A bridges high and pushes off of his right foot until he can swing his right leg over B.
    139b—A comes back onto his knees and quickly slides his left arm through between his body and B's as in the preceding maneuver.

*Method Three*

140a—A scoops with his left knee (the leg B is Grapevining) and grabs the bottom of B's left foot with his right hand.

140b—A drives his left elbow against B's shinbone and pulls up on B's foot.

140c—A slides down between B's legs with his buttocks and turns into B.

*Method Four*

141a—When B is attempting to get a "Guillotine," A straightens his arm forward.

141b—A grasps B's left wrist and bridges back against B's arm. When A has forced B's arm out and flattened B's chest to the mat, A releases B's wrist and turns into him. A now has a Cross Body ride on B. (A keeps B's left leg hooked with the heel of his left foot to prevent B from stepping across into a Top Body Scissors.)

# ESCAPES FROM SPECIAL RIDES

*Escape from Crab Ride*

142—A bridges back into B, pushes down on B's right knee with his right hand until he can slide his buttocks over B's right knee. A shoots his legs out perpendicular to B and turns toward B's legs.

*Escape from Stretcher*

It is easier to effect an Escape from the Cross Body Scissors than it is from a Stretcher. A "starts moving" before B gets him flattened out.

> 143a—A should keep his elbows close to his body, scoop with his right knee against B's right ankle, and curl himself up until B is forced onto his buttocks.
> 143b—A proceeds from this point in the same manner as described in Method Three for Escaping from the Cross Body Ride.

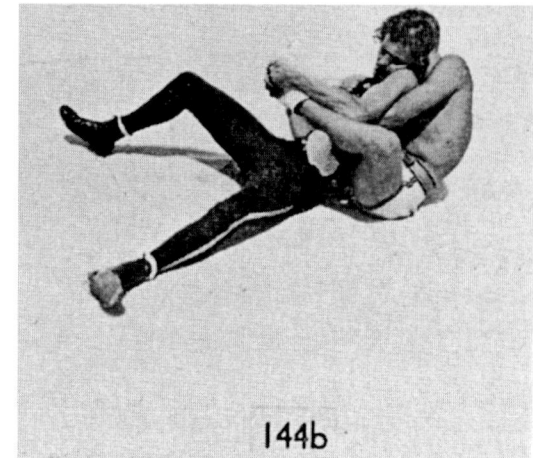

## Escape from Figure Four Scissors

144a—A keeps his elbows in close to his body, steps over B's "long" leg with his left knee, and rolls to his left side.

144b—A grabs the bottom of B's left foot (the long leg), with his right hand, pulls up, drives his left elbow against B's shin bone and proceeds in the same manner as suggested in Method Three for Escaping from a Cross Body Ride.

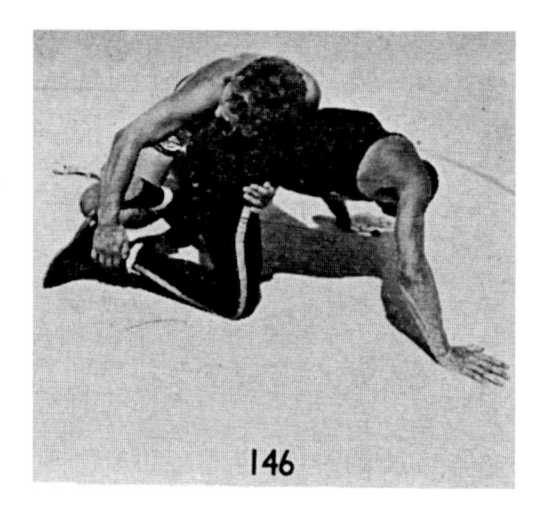

## Escapes from Ankle Ride

### Method One

145—A pushes back into B, settling on his left buttock. A grasps B's right wrist with his right hand and straightens out his right leg. (From this position, A follows up with a Stand Up, Side Roll, Sit Out or some other Escape.)

### Method Two

146—A drives forward, kicks with his left foot against B's right wrist, thereby freeing his right foot from B's grasp. (A follows quickly with a Stand Up, Sit Out, or some other Escape.)

## ESCAPES FROM SPECIAL RIDES

*Escape from Over Leg Ride*

147a—When B is Riding with his right leg hooked around A's left leg, A stands up quickly, thus locking B's right ankle against the instep of A's left foot.

147b—A pivots on his left foot, drives his left knee into B, forcing B to fall backward onto his buttocks. A follows up by dropping on B in a position of advantage.

CHAPTER XIV

# Counters for Common Methods of Escape

It is imperative that Counters for all of the more common methods of Escape from Underneath be learned and practiced. The number one Counter is to keep your opponent off balance and broken down in a prone position. By doing this, most of his possibilities of Escape are eliminated and, equally important, you thereby may set up an opportunity for securing a fall. A common method of Riding is to employ a strictly Counter attack of operation, viz.: let the underneath man take the initiative and the one Riding merely block or Counter all of his moves. The objection to this method of Riding is that the rules require the wrestler occupying the position of advantage to make a constant effort to secure a fall. If the underneath wrestler is making no effort to Escape, the one Riding may be penalized for "stalling."

*Counters for the Stand Up*
  *Method One*
    148—A rides B's legs and pulls up on the instep of the opposite foot on which B attempts to stand.

  *Method Two*
    149—As B starts to stand, A comes to his feet, locks his hands around B's waist, or obtains a Two on One Bar Lock on either of B's wrists. From this position, A takes B back down to the mat by any of the methods explained in Chapter VIII.

## Counters for the Sit Out

*Method One*

150a—A locks under both of B's arms, keeps his knees spread, and well up under him.

150b—A removes his left shoulder from underneath B's head, thereby eliminating B's support. A pulls B back under him with his right arm and secures an Arm Lock and Reverse Body Lock

*Method Two*

151a—A drives forward with his chest against B's head. A slips his hands down and catches inside of B's corresponding thighs.

151b—With his right hand, A reaches under B's right knee and pulls B backward into a Cradle (Jack Knife).

151c—A catches B's right heel with his right hand and the back of B's right leg with his left hand, drives his right leg over B's left leg and "cuts down." A can get tremendous pressure by applying this hold correctly; he has unlimited leverage on B's right leg.

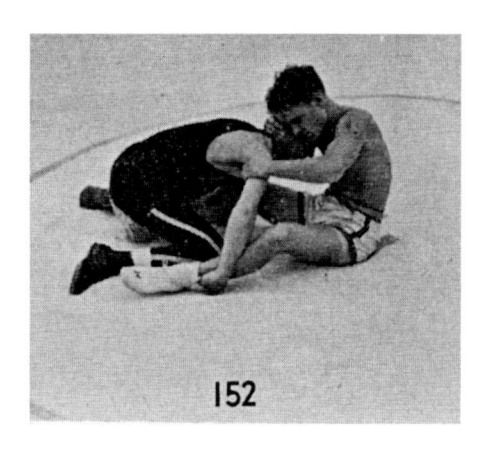

152

153

*Method Three*
  152—A drives forward with his chest against B's head with his hands catching inside of B's thighs in the same manner described in the preceding method. A pivots on his chest, swings around to B's front and picks up B's legs.

*Method Four*
  153—As B brings his knee off the mat to start sliding his legs forward, A locks his hands inside B's thighs, pulls B into him, and pulls B to one side or the other. A then flattens B to the mat with a Break Down.

154

**Counter for Power Craw Fish**
  154—A over-hooks B's right arm with his right arm when B reaches under. A comes out perpendicular to B and secures a Reverse Double Bar Arm Lock.

# COUNTERS FOR THE COMMON METHODS OF ESCAPE

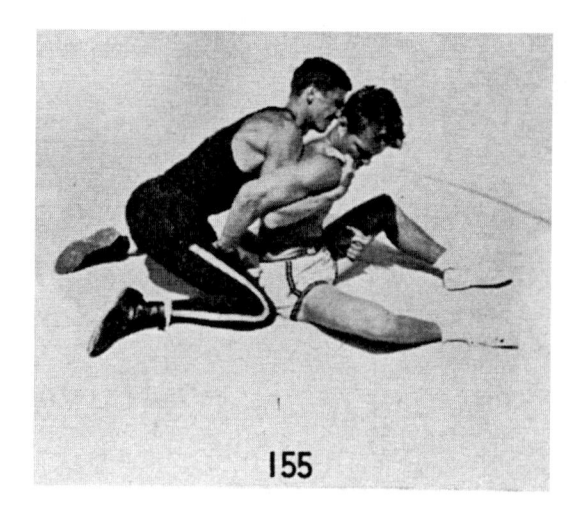

155

## Counters for the Switch
### Method One

155—A can block a Switch in the same manner as has been described in Method One for blocking a Sit Out, by driving forward and swinging his knees to the side opposite to which B is attempting the Switch. From this position, A catches under B's arms and pulls B backward. A then proceeds in the same manner as described for countering a Sit Out.

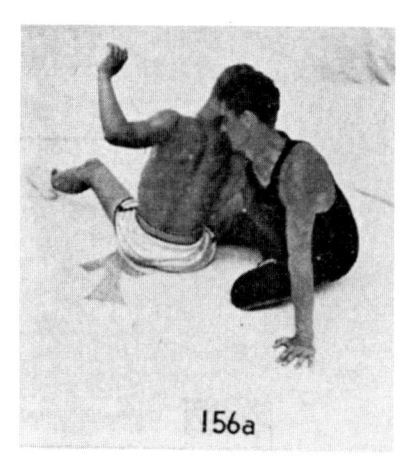

156a 156b 156c

### Method Two

156a—A common counter for a Switch is a "Re-switch." When B starts his Switch, he has put A in the same position for Switching that A occupies.

156b—As B switches to A's right, A swings through with B and comes on top of B again.

156c—At this point, it is advisable for A to give B a "limp arm" which enables A to remove the arm lever held by B.

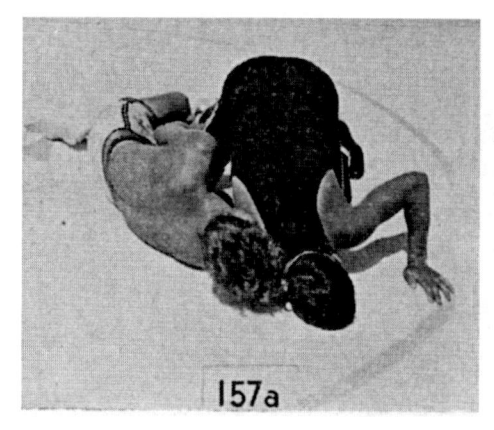

*Method Three*

157a—A Leg Step Over is also commonly used to counter a Switch. When B starts a Switch to the right, A locks over B's right arm with a Wing Lock.

157b—A drives his right shoulder to the mat and swings his legs across B's body. Use of this Counter often places A in a good position for Pinning B, as A has B's arm locked and has B on his back.

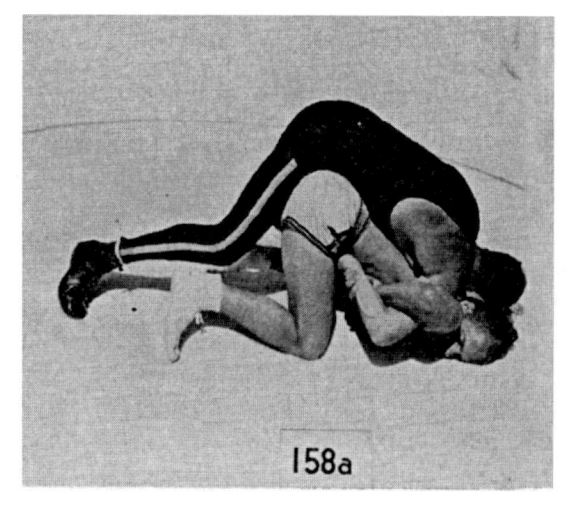

**Counters for a Double Wrist Lock**

*Method One*

158a—When B secures A's right wrist for a Double Wrist Lock, *A drives into B* and pivots over to B's right side with his knees up under him for a good base.

158b—A locks his hands in a wrestler's grip and pulls up, thereby breaking B's Double Wrist Lock. A follows up with a Half Nelson.

*Method Two*

159—A drives into B and swings across in the same manner as described in Method One. A straightens his right arm, catches inside of his own right thigh, sags his buttocks, and pushes hard with his chest. A stays perpendicular to B and keeps his weight distributed to prevent B reversing with a Double Wrist Wing Lock.

*Method Three*

160—A lifts on the instep of B's left foot, drives B onto his right shoulder and pushes him forward at an angle of 45 degrees, thereby breaking B's Double Wrist Lock.

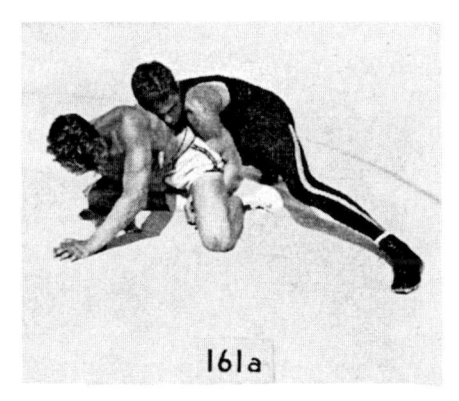

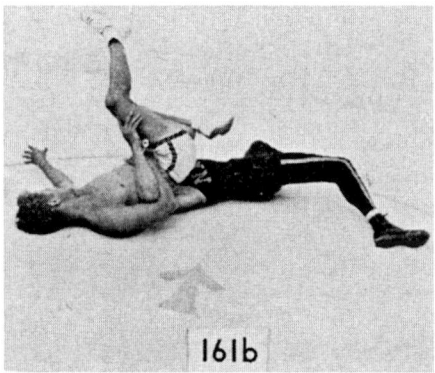

*Counter for the Side Roll*

*Method One*

161a—When B attempts a Side Roll to the right side, A takes a Rear Crotch hold with his left hand.

161b—A lifts on B's crotch and rolls through with B.

161c—A comes on top of B again.

162

*Method Two*

162—Countering this hold is a matter of balance and keeping the weight distributed properly. A should sag with his buttocks and reach for a Half Nelson on the left side when B is attempting to roll A to B's right.

163

**Counter for the Elevator**

163—A should keep his arms inside of B's arms and *stay off of B's elevator*. A maintains his support *on his own knees*, keeps his legs on the outside of B and does *not work too high on B*. A endeavors to depend upon his own base for support. A keeps his center of gravity located at his buttocks. A must be alert to take an Inside Crotch Ride on B.

CHAPTER XV

# Method for Giving Class Instruction

Giving class instruction and training a team for competition in wrestling are quite different. In class instruction it is necessary to present your material in a standardized manner and, more or less, in the nature of drills. In a wrestling class of cadets you are not primarily concerned in developing an individual but in teaching the rudiments of the sport to the entire group. It is necessary to gauge your instruction to suit the receptive ability of the slower members of the class rather than to develop the few individuals of outstanding ability.

For efficient teaching, *it is absolutely necessary* to have a carefully prepared lesson plan. In preparing your daily lesson plans, you must know the number of class periods and the length of time for each. Fortified with this information, you should exercise the greatest care in preparing a teaching schedule for the entire term, with definite daily lesson plans. The Navy slogan, "Plan your work and work your plan," is particularly significant and necessary to obtain maximum results in teaching a class in wrestling.

On the first day the first ten minutes should be devoted to explaining the highlights of the rules, the general purpose and objectives in wrestling, and the general rules of conduct and procedure you intend to maintain in conducting the class. Do not attempt "to tell the whole story" the first day; it will take up too much time. More details can be supplied and worked in during subsequent periods. *Do not ramble.* Have your remarks reduced to clear, simple and understandable statements.

### *Raised Instruction Platform*

In conducting a large class it is desirable to demonstrate from a raised platform. It should be approximately two feet high and ten feet square. It should be placed at the side, equidistant from the extremities of the wrestling area. It must be well padded to enable the instructor to give a realistic demonstration without fear of getting hurt. Any member of the class may be used on which to demonstrate, preferably one of the more advanced students. If you have assistants working with you, they can be of more use in observing and helping to correct those who are having difficulty than as sparring partners to the instructor.

### *The Whistle*

All maneuvers should start and stop with the sound of the whistle. The class must be made to understand that you intend to have the whistle "speak with authority." Some members of the class will be inclined to continue with their

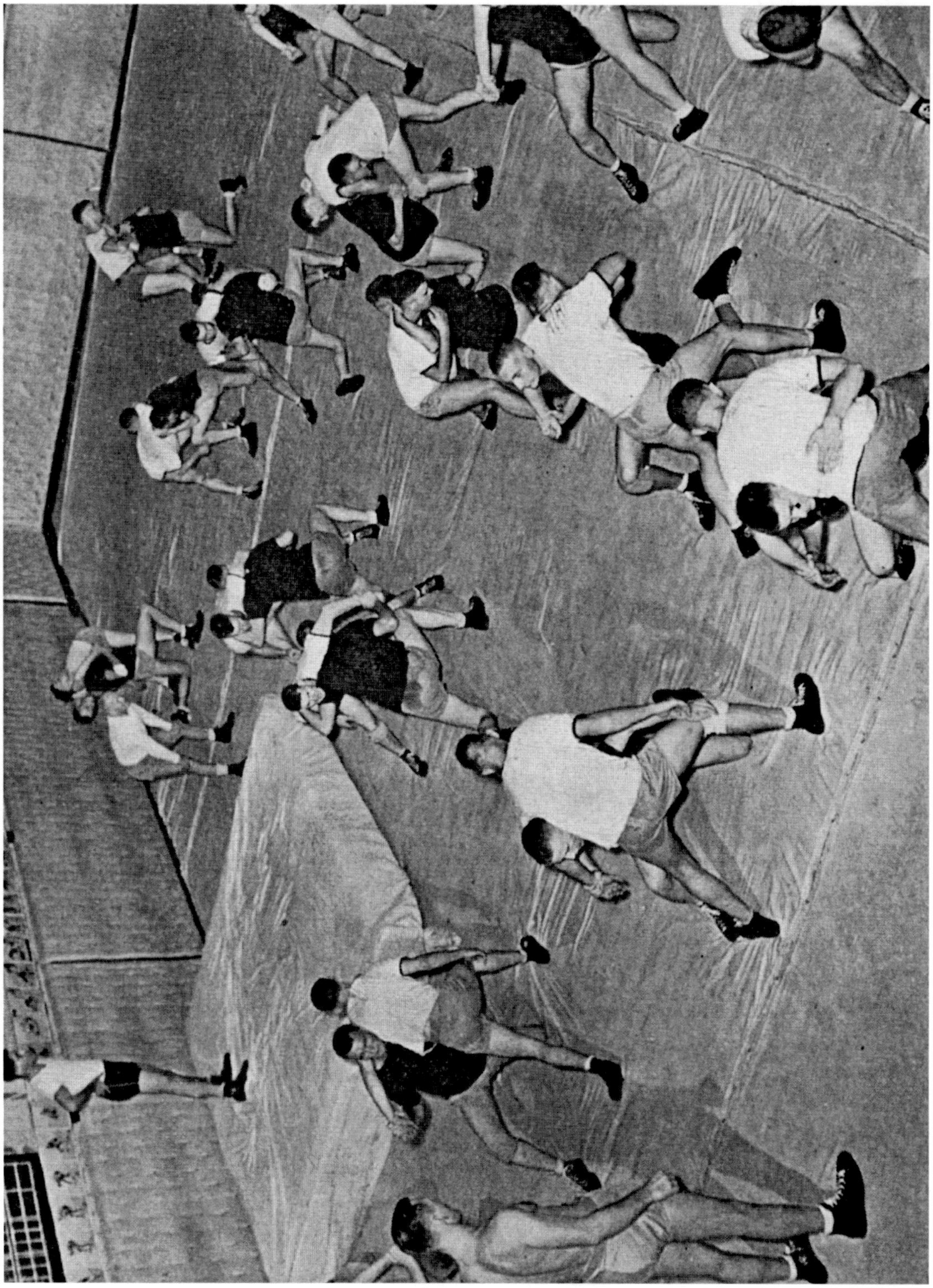

experimentations after the whistle blows, but this cannot be permitted. Efficient teaching requires that all members of the group perform the same operation together.

*The Warm-Up*

About five minutes at the beginning of each class should be devoted to calisthenics and warming up exercises. Wrestling has many body moves and shiftings which may profitably be used for warming up. The routines which develop definite wrestling maneuvers should be used to serve a two-fold purpose of warming up and reviewing fundamental techniques. The following routines are suggested, all to be executed vigorously and with speed:

*Mat Drill.*—This drill consists of having the men change quickly from one announced position to another. "Up" (Standing), "Back" (On their backs), "Stomach" (On their stomachs), "Right" (On their right sides), "Left" (On their left sides), and "Running in Place," are the commands to be given. They can be given in any desired order. Quickly changing from one of these announced positions to another is splendid for warming up, testing alertness, and developing speed in reaction.

*Bridging.*—Supine lying; arch back so that head and feet are the supporting points. Swing arms in various directions and pivot on your head without the use of hands in turning over.

*Push-ups.*—The hands and feet are the supporting points; keep body rigid and push up from a prone position on the mat until the arms are fully extended. Real zest can be added to this exercise by extending the arms with such force that the body is propelled upward, allowing the hands to be clapped together before starting the downward movement again. Pushing up with one arm with the other folded behind the back is another strenuous exercise very effective for developing arm strength.

*Rocking.*—From a prone position the back is arched until the body is entirely supported on the stomach. From this position, rock back and forth. Excellent for development of the trunk muscles.

*Abdominal Exercise.*—Supine lying; slowly raise both feet until the legs are in a vertical position, then slowly let them down to the mat again.

*Floating.*—From referee's position on the mat; top man supports his weight by resting his chest on under man's back. Under man attempts to maneuver in any manner he desires with top man attempting to control his own balance and prevent opponent's escape without either applying wrestling holds.

*Switching.*—From referee's position on the mat; alternating with inside and outside Switches against semi-resistance. See page 97.

*Sit Outs.*—From referee's position on the mat; under man drives his head backward and propels his feet out in front of him and makes a quick turn either way onto his knees. From here, he should quickly complete a reversal by hopping behind opponent with a Snap Down, Short Arm Drag, Cross Face or some other appropriate maneuver. Opponent must use only semiresistance. See page 95.

*Modified Combat Games*

The following modified combat games are adapted from wrestling techniques. These are designed to add interest, enthusiasm and variety to practice sessions as well

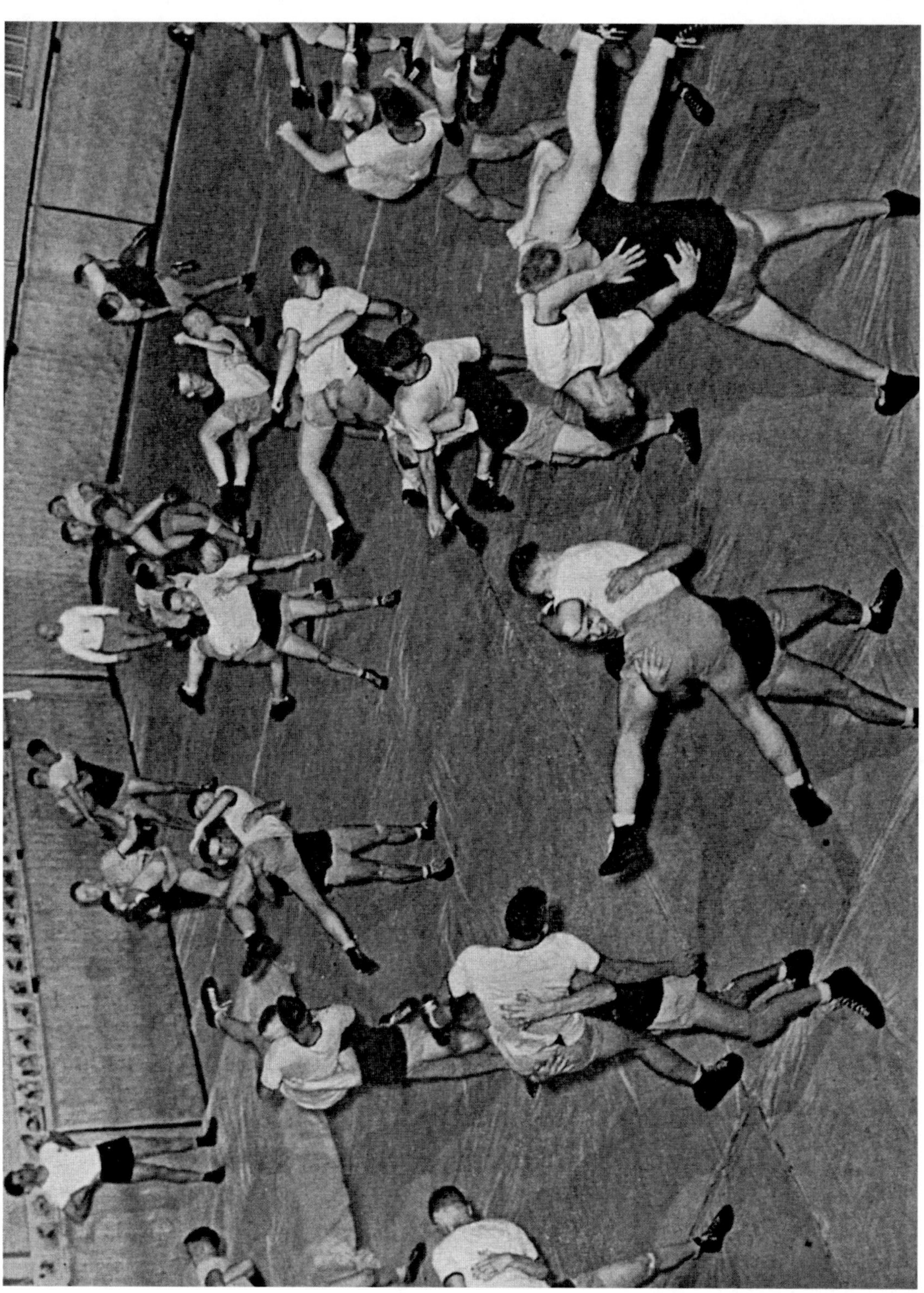

as to aid in the development of balance, leverage, body control and competitive spirit. They can be taught to a large group and many can be taught even when using limited facilities. Most of these games can be used as individual, team, or group contests.

*Collar and Elbow Wrestling.*—The right hand of each wrestler grasps his opponent's left elbow, while his left hand is placed on opponent's neck. The object is to make an opponent touch the ground with any part of his body other than the feet.

*Side Hold Wrestling.*—Each man places his right arm around the opponent's waist and grasps the opponent's right elbow with his left hand. The object is to make the opponent touch the mat with some part of his body other than his feet.

*Indian Wrestling.*—Wrestlers face each other, grasp the opponent's right hand, and place the outside edge of their right feet together. The object is to make an opponent move a foot or touch the mat with hand or knee.

*Standing Arm Drag to Gain Advantage.*—The object is to gain standing position of advantage behind an opponent by the use of the Arm Drag (for more detail see page 34).

*Ring Wrestle.*—Opponents attempt to force each other out of the circle.

*Leg Wrestle.*—Wrestlers lie side by side on back with heads in opposite directions. Hook right elbows. On count of one, raise right legs and touch together, repeat on two; on three, hook legs and attempt to turn the other over into a backward roll.

*Rooster Fight.*—In a circle two opponents grasp their own left foot with the right hand and grip right arm with the left hand behind the back. They hop at each other and try to force their opponent out of a circle or cause him to lose his balance.

*Sparrow Fight.*—Two wrestlers, grasping their own ankles, attempt to push each other out of a circle.

*Shoulder Shove.*—Wrestlers stand on one leg, arms folded, use shoulders to shove opponent out of ring, or to lose his balance.

*Hop Fight.*—Two persons in a circle, arms folded, raise one leg in front. The object is to force the other from the circle or to upset him by use of lifted leg only.

*Twist Stick.*—Face opponent in a standing position, arms extended over head, grasping a stick with both hands. The object is to lower the stick, retaining grip and cause stick to turn in opponent's hands.

*Stick Wrestle.*—Two wrestlers grasp stick. The object is to wrestle the stick from opponent. (Two short sticks can also be used, grasping one in each hand.)

*Medicine Ball Wrestle.*—Opponents face one another, each grasping a basketball held chest high between them. The object is to wrest the ball from opponent.

*Bulldog Pull.*—Opponents face each other on hands and knees with a strap (two belts) looped over their heads. The object is to pull opponent across a line.

*Horse and Rider Wrestling.*—Each wrestler is mounted on another wrestler as

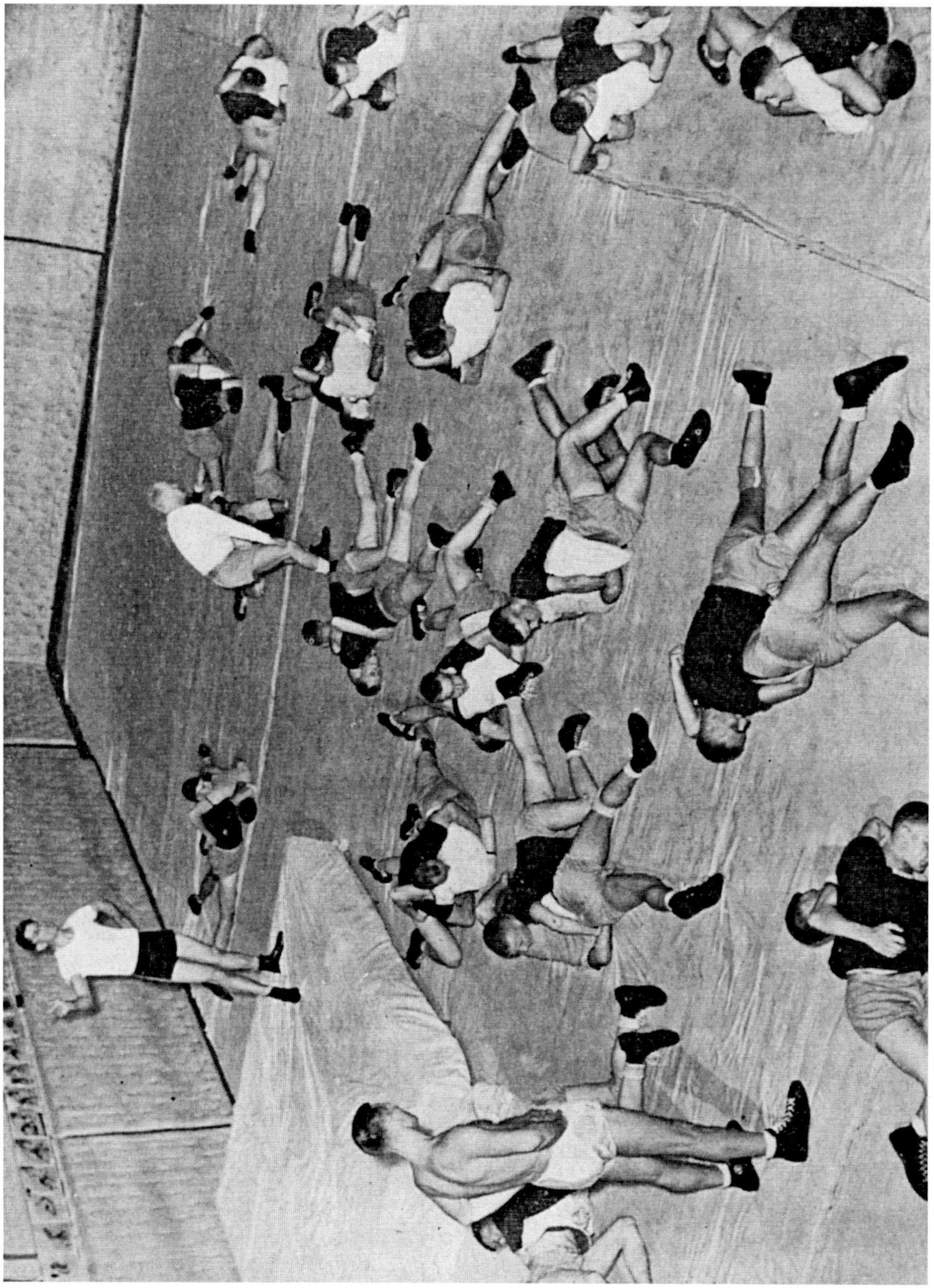

horse and rider. The "horse" may stand erect or for greater safety be placed on hands and knees. The object is to unseat the rider.

*King of the Mats.*—1. Each team appoints a king which they attempt to maintain in power by occupying a specified area of the mat. Opposing team attempts by pulling, pushing, and wrestling to force opposing "king" from throne area and placing their own "king" there instead.

2. A second method is for each team to attempt to throw all opposing team members out of a given mat area. The team having the greater number within the specified area after a given time is the winner.

*Pull Over Line.*—Two teams are arranged across a line from each other. The object is to grasp an opponent and pull him across the line.

*Wrestle Royal.*—Any number can take part. Each contestant for himself. Members may "gang up" on individuals. Those thrown are eliminated until an ultimate winner is determined. (This may also be used as a team contest.)

*Take Down Wrestling.*—The members of the class shall be lined up, graduated according to weight. Have them "count off" by eights or tens, depending upon the size of the class. The "odds" shall take positions in groups of fours or fives on one side of the mat area, to be opposed by the "even" groups who take their positions on the other side of the mat area. These groups shall likewise line up, graduated according to weight, with the lighter men in the "odd" group opposing the lighter men in the "even" group for their first match.

The objective is to get a Take Down and retain a controlling position until the referee designates him to be the winner. The loser retires to the side line and the winner remains to meet the next challenger. None of the contestants will be permitted to engage in more than two matches. The group having a man, or men, remaining when all of the members from the opposing group have been defeated is the winner.

This same game can be repeated by reversing the order of the bouts, viz.; have the heavier men of each group oppose each other first and continue with the elimination in the same manner.

*Knee Slap.*—This game teaches balance, body control, and at the same time increases speed of reaction.

Activity starts from a closed stance with each wrestler grasping the neck of his opponent with the right hand allowing the left hand to dangle at his side. (This position may be reversed with the left hand on the neck and the right hand at the side.) The contestants should bend well forward at the waist, lower the hips by bending the knees slightly and maintain their weight on the balls of their feet. The position should be a comfortable one.

1. Do not lean too far forward.
2. Do not be back on your heels.
3. Do not stand too straight.

The object from now on is to slap either of opponent's knees with the free hand. The winner of the game will be the one who slaps his opponent's knee three out of five or the best of any series.

The movement of the feet should be such that they will maintain balance at all times. Movements for the most part will be a series of short hops on both feet. If steps are taken forward or to the side, they should be very short, and feet should never be crossed.

### "No Fall" Wrestling

"No Fall" Wrestling had its origin in England and was called "Standing Catch Can" by its originator Mr. S. V. Bacon. Lifting an opponent so that both his feet are clear of the ground constitutes the basis for scoring a victory. Contestants are not permitted to touch the ground with any part of their bodies excepting their feet without penalty.

Competition may be carried on almost any place with disregard for facilities and equipment.

It must be understood, however, that it is only a sub-division of real standing wrestling and cannot be substituted for even that branch.

Many couples can participate at one time. It lends opportunity for a good competitive, vigorous workout. It is an excellent "warming up" activity with incentive and interest.

*Rules.*—The rules of the game are few and simple.

1. Area—any smooth surface.

2. Costume—a gymnasium outfit.

3. Point scoring:
   *Lift*—3 points.
   Lifting both feet clear of the ground.
   *Partial Lift*—1 point.
   Both feet off the ground but one or both legs interlocked with opponent's legs.
   *Deliberate Falling*—3 points to opponent.
   Deliberate falling to avoid a lift.
   *Accidental Falling or Slipping to the ground*—1 point to opponent.
   *Deliberate Throw*—3 points to opponent.

4. Length of Match—The duration of match is limited to five minutes.

5. Winner
1. Contestant scoring most points.
2. The first contestant to secure a lift. In the event there is no lift, the contestant scoring the greater number of points.
3. In case of tie score, the bout is declared a draw. An extra period of two minutes duration may be permitted.

Attack Maneuvers—Pictures and Positions Numbers 1; 2; 9; 29a, b; 32a, b, c; 41a, b, c; 53a, b; 59a and 61a.

Defense and Counter Attack—Numbers 7; 11; 30a; 36a; 60a; 61a.

# INSTRUCTIONS FOR THE CONDUCT OF A CLASS TOURNAMENT

The brackets outlined on the following pages offer a method of determining place winners in each weight division of eight men. These methods were developed in the Naval Aviation Physical Training Program as a convenient, simple and time-saving means for conducting class tournaments.

1. Class members are arranged in a single line formation, graduated according to weight, with the heaviest man on the right and the lightest man on the left end of the line.
2. Class counts off by eights.
3. Odds step out two paces and face the man to their left who will be their opponents for the first match.
4. The number eight man is responsible for having each man in his group fill in the bracket form which has been given to him. Each man should list his name, initials, and actual weight.
5. After the brackets are filled in, an explanation of the method of conducting the tournament should be given. An enlarged drawing of the bracket is a convenient aid in making his explanation more clear.
6. The men in the top half of the bracket should wrestle first and the men in the lower half of the bracket can be utilized to officiate.
7. All of the matches (in the upper bracket) should start together. These matches should be limited to approximately 3 minutes.
8. When a match is concluded by a fall the winners should retire to one bulkhead and the losers to another. If no fall occurs within 3 minutes the referee decides the winner.
9. The lower half of the bracket should be wrestled in an identical manner, with men in the upper bracket officiating.
10. After this preliminary round, the winners will wrestle the winners and the losers against the losers.
11. The brackets shown on the following pages are self explanatory.
12. In Form I, the champion will be determined by elimination of the winners of each progressive round. Similarly, the *"chumpion"* will be determined by having the losers of each progressive round matched.
13. A consolation tournament can also be run very conveniently, and at the same time, by matching the first round winners in the *"Chumpionship"* bracket against the second round losers in the Championship bracket.
14. In Form II, winners of the first round advance to the right and losers to the left. Elimination is conducted on the right side bracket to determine the Champion; the defeated finalist is runner-up. The winner of the left side bracket wins third place; the defeated finalist of the left side bracket wins fourth place.

Advantages of this complete elimination are:
1. More objective method of grading.
2. Each man will have at least three matches.

# WRESTLING

## FORM I

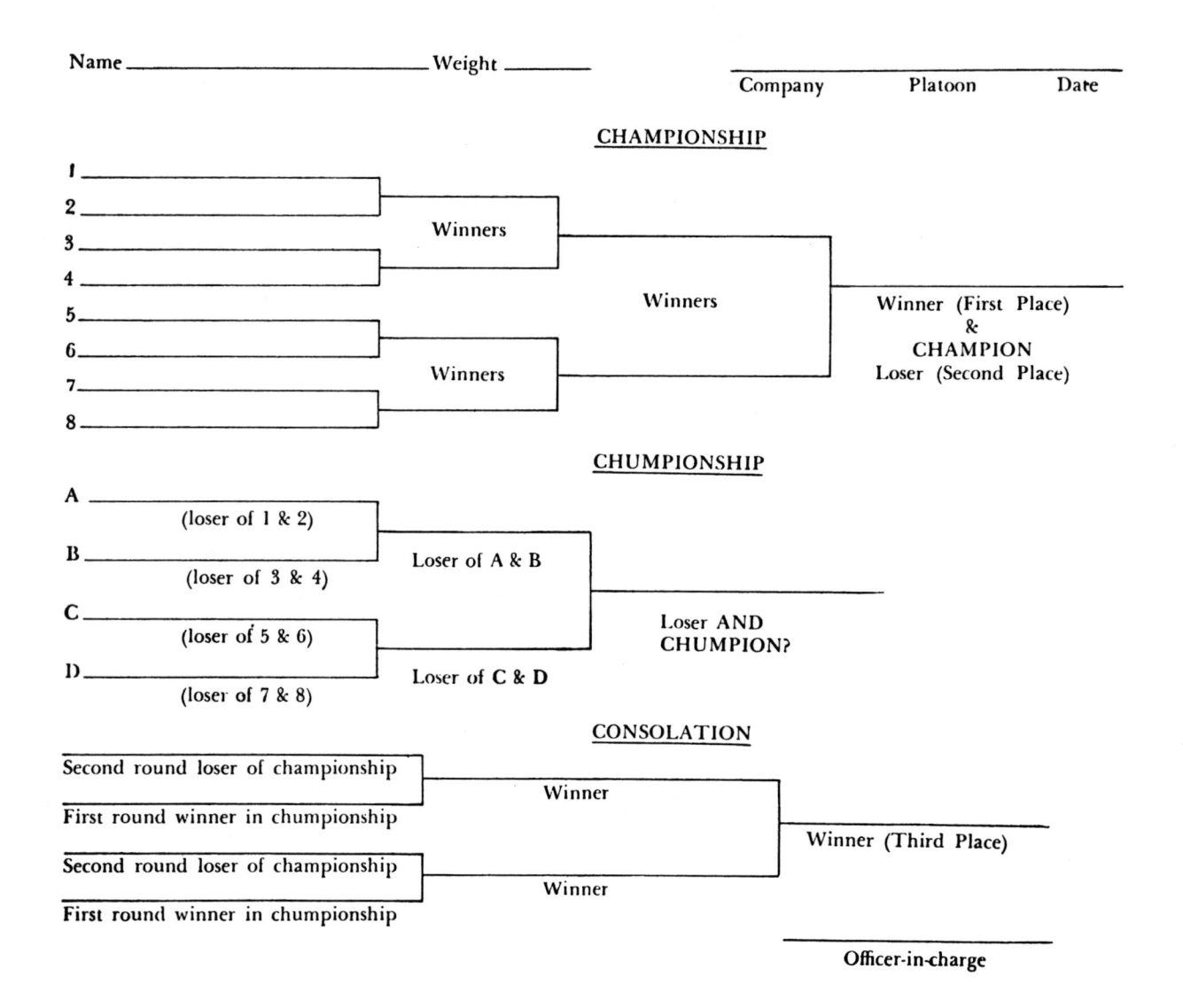

Name _____ Weight _____    _____
                                      Company    Platoon    Date

### CHAMPIONSHIP

```
1 ─┐
2 ─┴─ Winners ─┐
3 ─┐           ├─ Winners ─┐
4 ─┴─ Winners ─┘           ├── Winner (First Place)
5 ─┐                       │   &
6 ─┴─ Winners ─┐           │   CHAMPION
7 ─┐           ├─ Winners ─┘   Loser (Second Place)
8 ─┴─ Winners ─┘
```

### CHUMPIONSHIP

```
A ─┐ (loser of 1 & 2)
   ├─ Loser of A & B ─┐
B ─┘ (loser of 3 & 4)  │
                       ├── Loser AND
C ─┐ (loser of 5 & 6)  │   CHUMPION?
   ├─ Loser of C & D ─┘
D ─┘ (loser of 7 & 8)
```

### CONSOLATION

```
Second round loser of championship ─┐
                                    ├─ Winner ─┐
First round winner in chumpionship ─┘          │
                                               ├── Winner (Third Place)
Second round loser of championship ─┐          │
                                    ├─ Winner ─┘
First round winner in chumpionship ─┘
```

_____
Officer-in-charge

## FORM II

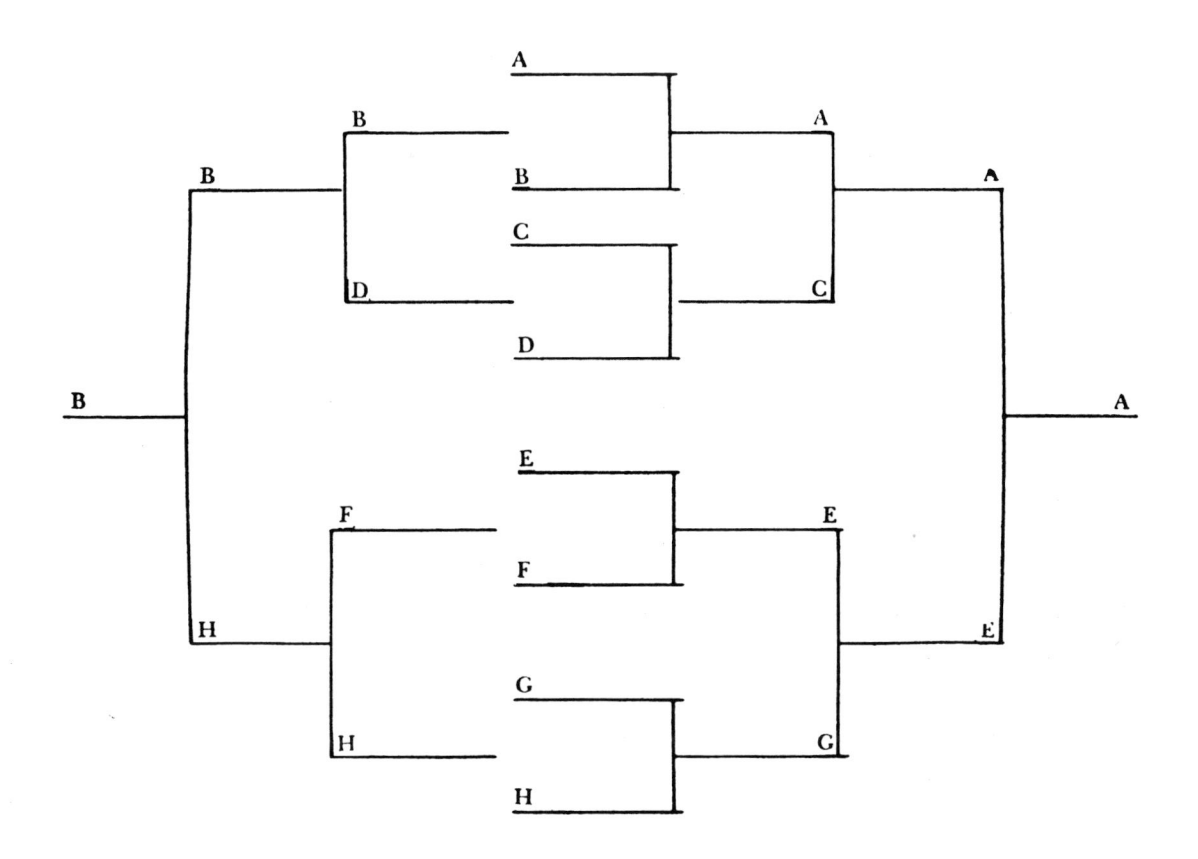

A—Champion
E—Runner-up
B—Consolation winner
H—Fourth place winner

## SCORE SHEETS

It is desirable to keep score sheets for all try-out matches as well as dual meet or tournament matches. This record can be used for the information of the coach as well as the contestant in the correction of mistakes and in the preparation for future matches.

The following forms are included to represent different methods which may be used to record pertinent information.

## PRACTICE MATCHES

DATE _____

WEIGHT _____ CONTESTANT: _____

|  | T. Down | Reverse | Nearfall | Escapes | T. Adv. | Tot. Pts. |
|---|---|---|---|---|---|---|
| 1st Period |  |  |  |  |  |  |
| 2nd Period |  |  |  |  |  |  |
| 3rd Period |  |  |  |  |  |  |
| Totals |  |  |  |  |  |  |

CONTESTANT: _____

|  | T. Down | Reverse | Nearfall | Escapes | T. Adv. | Tot. Pts. |
|---|---|---|---|---|---|---|
| 1st Period |  |  |  |  |  |  |
| 2nd Period |  |  |  |  |  |  |
| 3rd Period |  |  |  |  |  |  |
| Totals |  |  |  |  |  |  |

| NAME | Take Downs | Revs. | Esc. | Near Falls | Falls | Time Wres. | T.A. | Remarks |
|---|---|---|---|---|---|---|---|---|
| 1. | | | | | | | | |
| 2. | | | | | | | | |
| 3. | | | | | | | | |
| 4. | | | | | | | | |
| 5. | | | | | | | | |
| 6. | | | | | | | | |
| 7. | | | | | | | | |
| 8. | | | | | | | | |
| 9. | | | | | | | | |
| 10. | | | | | | | | |
| 11. | | | | | | | | |
| 12. | | | | | | | | |
| 13. | | | | | | | | |
| 14. | | | | | | | | |
| 15. | | | | | | | | |
| 16. | | | | | | | | |

**WRESTLING TRIAL SCORE SHEET**

# WRESTLING

DATE _____

| NAME | WT | TAKE DOWNS | REVS. | ESC. | NEAR FALLS | FALLS | TIME WRES. | T.A. | REMARKS |
|------|----|-----|------|------|------|------|------|------|---------|
|  |  |  |  |  |  |  |  |  |  |
|  |  |  |  |  |  |  |  |  |  |

**TRYOUT MATCHES**

| Bout No | Weight Class | Contestants | Team | MATCH POINTS ||||||| Winner Team | Fall or Dec'n Hold Used | Time of Fall | Team Points |
| | | | | Take-Downs | Escapes | Reversals | Near-Falls | Time Adv. | Totals | | | | |
| 1 | | | | | | | | | | | | | |
| 2 | | | | | | | | | | | | | |
| 3 | | | | | | | | | | | | | |
| 4 | | | | | | | | | | | | | |
| 5 | | | | | | | | | | | | | |
| 6 | | | | | | | | | | | | | |
| 7 | | | | | | | | | | | | | |
| 8 | | | | | | | | | | | | | |
| 9 | | | | | | | | | | | | | |
| 10 | | | | | | | | | | | | | |

| Score by Bout | TEAMS | 1 | 2 | 3 | 4 | 5 | 6 | 7 | 8 | 9 | 10 | Bouts Won | Bouts Lost | Bouts Tied | Final Score |
|---|---|---|---|---|---|---|---|---|---|---|---|---|---|---|---|
| | | | | | | | | | | | | | | | |
| | | | | | | | | | | | | | | | |

Held At _____ vs. _____ Date _____ Attendance _____

REFEREE _____  HEAD SCORER _____  RECORDER _____

HEAD TIMER _____  TIMER _____  TIMER _____

DUAL WRESTLING MEET

# SUGGESTIONS TO REFEREES

By Clifford P. Keen

Member, NCAA Wrestling Rules Committee

*Reprint from NCAA Official Wrestling Guide (By Permission)*

There is no such thing as a "perfect" referee in wrestling. In the first place, there is perhaps no group of coaches in the land who are in perfect agreement on their interpretations of rules and in accord on their evaluations and judgment as to what constitutes superior wrestling ability. It follows that the decisions of a good referee, whose judgment and knowledge of wrestling is as expert as either of the coaches, may be at variance with one or the other or both of the coaches. Add to this factor the natural prejudice which a coach has for one of his own boys and his "wishful thinking" as to meritorious performances which he is inclined to attribute to his own protege during the course of a bout, and the referee has "two strikes against him," regardless of what kind of officiating he does.

However, there are several important qualities which a referee must possess to enable him to do a capable job of refereeing. First, he must KNOW THE RULES. The rules should be read and studied until the referee is thoroughly familiar with each detail of every provision. He should visualize the operation of each and every provision, so that his judgment may be instantaneous and correct when he gets to the actual task of officiating. Before accepting an assignment, he should get in a lot of practice by visiting a wrestling room and refereeing practice matches. It is also highly desirable that clinics be arranged before the season gets underway to enable a group discussion of rules and a composite interpretation of all provisions, with both referees and coaches in attendance.

In addition to having a thorough knowledge of the rules, it is necessary for a referee to have a thorough knowledge of wrestling. He must be cognizant of the technical aspect of wrestling holds; he must understand wrestling from the wrestler's point of view; he must have the judgment to carry out the spirit of the rules, together with a common-sense interpretation; he should be familiar with various styles of wrestling and have the ability to understand and appraise the significance of various maneuvers which are used.

Some of the most difficult decisions which must be made arise from situations occurring at the edge of the mat. In this connection, sound discretion must be exercised in determining whether or not control was obtained while the supporting points of either wrestler was on the mat; whether wrestler A was pushed off by B or whether A got off the mat to prevent a take down by B or if in a defensive position, to prevent being pinned.

The determining factor for awarding points for a Take Down is control. This important decision is entirely up to the discretion of the referee, so be sure that you understand thoroughly what constitutes control. In Escapes, the Escapee should not be awarded a point until he is definitely free. In Reverses the Reverser should not be awarded two (2) points until he has definitely effected control over the Reversee.

Good judgment and sound discretion must be exercised in the inflicting of penalties and the determination of illegal holds. The general rule which prohibits the "use of any hold for punishment alone" or the use of any hold "that endangers life or limb" gives the referee a wide range of discretion, so his judgment must be sound and his discretion exercised with wisdom and understanding.

Consistency is the golden virtue of a good referee. Calling a decision one way on one occasion and differently on another under similar circumstances can easily lead to confusion and result in an injustice to the contestants. Don't be a "baseball umpire" by endeavoring to make up for a decision that you think you may have called wrong. In any close match, there are apt to be many close situations in which a decision must be made. Be prepared to meet them in a friendly, yet in a positive and authoritative manner.

The referee should be dressed in a neat-appearing uniform. The accepted dress consists of white or light-colored trousers, a "clean" white sport shirt or regular dress white shirt with a dark bow tie, and with neat gymnasium shoes. Don't try to be the "big show." The probability is that the spectators are paying to see the contestants perform and not the referee.

Make all announcements in a clear voice and in a positive manner. When points are awarded, they should be announced clearly and definitely, with appropriate gestures being given to signify exactly what the decision is.

Never be guilty of letting the match get out of your control. There have been some sad situations in which the referee has become so confused that he has rendered himself utterly incapable of performing his duty in an efficient manner. Sometimes this may be caused by fatigue, especially in tournaments where there are no relief referees provided. It is highly desirable to have more than two referees in any large tournament so as to prevent this possibility. Another serious possibility exists, with varying degrees of severity in different sections of the country, and that is the behavior of the spectators and of different coaches. The referee must be absolutely aloof and impregnable to any sort of intimidation. Any referee who permits the conduct of the spectators or the complaining of a coach to influence his decision is certainly not a competent person to be entrusted with the high responsibility to which he has been assigned. The referee should certainly not show a belligerent attitude toward the spectators, contestants or the coaches; but at the same time, he must be fortified with sufficient courage to require an atmosphere which is compatible with good sportsmanship and fair play. The referee should start (and finish) each match with absolutely no preconceived notions as to the relative ability of the two contestants; nor should any personal prejudice exist in his mind that would affect his decision in the slightest degree. So far as a good referee is concerned, one of the contestants wears "black" tights and the other wears "red" tights. The winner must be determined 100 percent on the basis of what he does on the mat in that particular match; he must be judged in accordance with an honest interpretation and an intelligent application of the rules.

CHAPTER XVI

# The Olympic Style of Wrestling

There is a marked contrast in the American amateur style of wrestling and the Olympic style of wrestling. Our wrestling is governed by the National Collegiate Athletic Association and the American Athletic Union rules, while the Olympic wrestling is governed by the International Amateur Wrestling Federation rules.

There are not only important differences in the rules, but also basic differences in the style, concept, philosophy, and objectives of the sport. First, in Olympic wrestling, they use the "touch" fall, viz., when points of both shoulders touch the mat simultaneously, it is considered a fall. In our style of wrestling it is necessary to hold an opponent's shoulders to the mat for a period of two seconds. This basic difference requires the use of radically different techniques. In our style of wrestling we may employ all sorts of maneuvers without fear of losing by having our shoulders touch the mat momentarily. In the European style of wrestling there must be a constant awareness and conservatism against the employment of any maneuver which may result in permitting the shoulders to touch. As a consequence of the "touch" fall, much of our advanced skill and knowledge leading to clever Take-Downs, Escapes, Riding (particularly with scissors holds), and Counter Attacks must either be abandoned or carefully adapted to cope with the situation. The Europeans employ a high Bridge which they consider to be indispensable in preventing the shoulders from touching the mat when on their backs. We do not need this tremendous neck development and proficiency, essential to the development of the Bridge, for successful performance in our style of wrestling.

Nor can we compete on even terms with the Europeans in strength. On the average, the European champions in wrestling are much older than our champions. They are in their early "thirties" while our champions are almost exclusively college men who are still in their early "twenties." As a result of these many years of experience and the added factor of their use of many supplemental physical development exercises, the Europeans are very definitely superior to us in strength. As a consequence of this important factor, we must depend on superior technique and cleverness to enable us to win.

The next most important distinguishing feature from our style of wrestling is their system of selecting the winner in those matches when a fall does not occur. In Olympic competition a "jury," is used, consisting of three judges and a referee.

The I.A.W.F. rules have no standardized method of evaluating credit points, such as we have, for the successful execution of Take-Downs, Escapes, Near-Falls, etc. The judges must use their own subjective powers in voting for the one they consider the better wrestler. Naturally, this often leads to an awkward situation in many of the close matches, especially since there is a great difference of opinion as to what constitutes superior wrestling ability. Generally speaking, however, nothing is particularly important or noteworthy in their concept except the nearness or effectiveness of the tactics employed by the contestants in the all important objective of securing a fall. To illustrate, "A" may have several Take-Downs and completely dominate "B" so far as control and "riding" are concerned, but if "B" should secure one "near-fall" or put "A" in one predicament where it would require a bit of doing to prevent being pinned, it is not unlikely that "B" would be judged the winner.

A Take-Down in itself means little or nothing unless it is followed up by some pinning effort. Likewise, riding or control of an opponent means nothing to them without some effective method being used toward tilting the underneath man onto his back. As a matter of fact, riding an opponent for a long period of time without making some headway toward getting a fall would be regarded as "passivity" and would actually count against one. By the same process of thinking, Escapes in themselves mean little or nothing unless followed by some effort to get a fall.

Carrying out this philosophy the referee does not draw fine distinctions in his decisions on the edge of the mat. Whereas we are particularly concerned whether the supporting points are on or off the mat in awarding a Take-Down, Reversal, or an Escape, they are somewhat indifferent since, to their way of thinking, it is quite immaterial anyway. This same attitude is also reflected to some extent in the European contestants. It does not seem to make much difference to them whether they are on their feet, underneath, or in a position of advantage. Most European wrestlers regard their possibilities of securing a fall to be just as good in one position as another.

Thus, this attitude of the European officials and wrestlers may explain the fact that our wrestlers have a marked superiority over the Europeans in Take-Downs, Escapes, and Riding. However, the average European is more proficient in getting falls and has a superior defense against getting pinned than the average American wrestler.

With this explanation of the European attitude and interpretation of the Olympic style of wrestling, some basic holds which can be used effectively in Olympic wrestling competition are described and illustrated. Only those holds which can lead directly to a fall will be considered in this chapter.

## STANDING

A favorite position of the European wrestler is to tie up with his opponent and to secure a Head and Arm Lock. From this position, by pulling and pushing, he undertakes to get his opponent off balance and to set up an opportunity to use either a Side Head Lock and Hip Throw or a Side Head Lock and Hip Throw Reverse as is illustrated below:

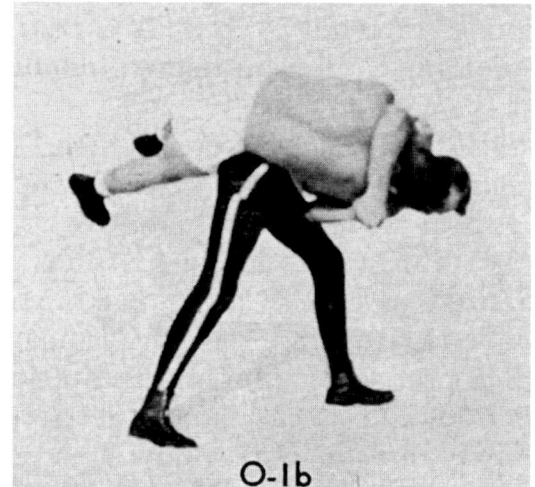

*Side Head Lock and Hip Throw*

*Side Head Lock and Hip Throw Reverse*

The Head Chancery and Double Bar arm and the Head Chancery and Hip Throw are also used in combination with each other. These holds are employed usually as a counter attack to Leg Tackles or Head Under Arm holds. However, they can also be initiated by maneuvering your opponent into a position where you can work his head under your arm.

*Head Chancery and Double Bar Arm*

*Head Chancery and Hip Throw*

**The Whip**
The Whip is a vicious and effective hold, peculiarly well adapted to the European style of wrestling. The secret of the hold is to trap your opponent into the error of permitting you to get both of his arms locked.

O-5a—A reaches with his right hand over B's left arm grasping above B's elbow. A drives his head under B's left arm, and grasps B's right wrist with his left hand in a reverse manner (with his thumb toward the extremity of B's hand). A hooks his left elbow underneath the crook of B's right arm.

O-5b—A pulls tightly, lifts up, pivots on his right foot and swings his left leg through, which will crash B to the mat in a pinning position.

## Elbow Lock and Hip Throw

This hold is quite innocent looking. Its success depends upon getting your opponent to attempt to step behind you into a Rear Body Lock position.

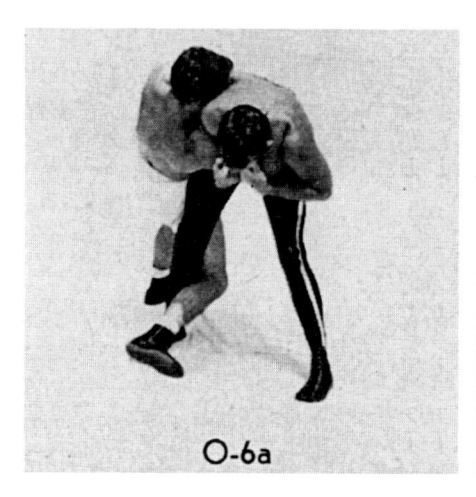

O-6a—When B places his right hand on A's neck A grasps at the crook of B's right arm with both of his hands. B may thus be enticed to endeavor to swing in behind A in what may appear to be a simple means of securing a Go Behind. As B starts his movement A steps through deeply behind B's right leg.

O-6b—A maintains his grasp on B's right arm and endeavors to touch B's shoulders to the mat as they fall.

## Double Arm Lock and Hip Throw

The Double Arm Lock and Hip Throw is not unlike our Whizzer (Over Arm Hook) hold.

O-7a—A overhooks B's left arm with his right arm. With his left hand A grasps B's right wrist, pulls up with his right arm, and secures a hook grip with his right hand on B's upper right arm.

O-7b—With this lock, A steps through deeply with his right foot and undertakes to touch B's shoulders as he falls to the mat.

## Head Under Arm Crotch Lift

This hold is quite feasible and effective against the European wrestler. The European is not trained to protect his legs to the same extent that we are in the American style of wrestling. For that reason it is not too difficult to work into a position to grasp one or both of his legs.

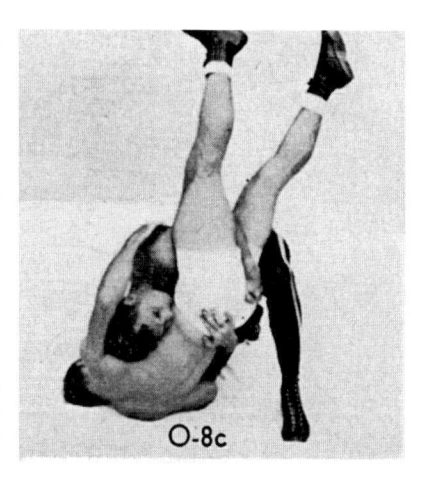

O-8a—A drives into B with his head lower than B's, steps deeply to the outside with his right foot, shifts his head under B's right arm, and lifts.

O-8b—It is imperative that A lift B free of the mat.

O-8c—A drops his right foot backward, shifts his right arm around B's waist, and brings B's shoulders to the mat in this locked position.

## Head Under Arm with Lateral Drag

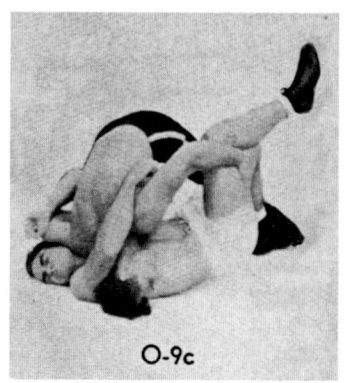

O-9a—A drives into B, grasps above B's left elbow with his right hand, and feints a move to grasp B's left leg.

O-9b—As B straightens his left leg, A jerks down on B's right arm, swings his right leg through to get added power, and swings his left arm high over B's back.

O-9c—A maintains his lock on B's left arm, takes advantage of his momentum, and drives B onto his shoulders for a fall.

# ESCAPES

## Down Position in Partere Wrestling

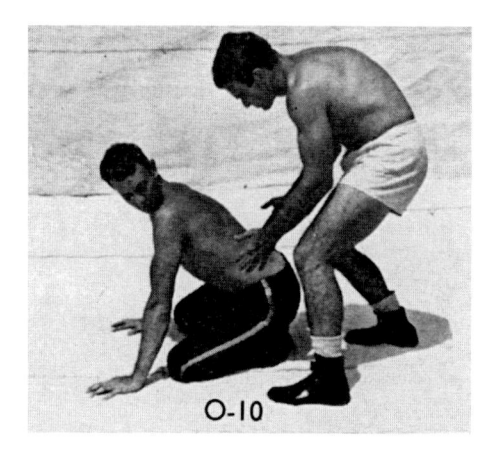

O-10—This represents a typical "down" position. Any position may be assumed so long as both knees and both hands are in contact with the mat. Inasmuch as great use is made of various forms of leg lifts in Olympic wrestling, it is advisable to have the feet well up under the buttocks, with the toes pointed either in or out so that the weight will be resting on the sides of the feet.

## The Wing Lock

Greater use is made of Wing Locks and Side Roll maneuvers than any other type of Escapes in Olympic wrestling. The reason for this is because a Wing Lock offers a good

THE OLYMPIC STYLE OF WRESTLING 145

opportunity to secure a fall or at least to put your opponent in a predicament. Since an Escape in itself counts for little in the Olympic style of wrestling, only those holds which are designed to secure a fall as the connected and ultimate objective should be used.

O-11a

O-11b

O-11c

*Single Wing Lock with Leg Lift*

O-11a—A grasps B's right wrist with his right hand. A pulls B's right elbow below B's right hip.

O-11b—A lunges forward, reaches above B's left upper arm with his left hand, and elevates B with his left leg.

O-11c—A bridges back into B, with his legs perpendicular to B's body, and endeavors to touch B's shoulders to the mat for a fall.

*Near Side Double Wing Lock*

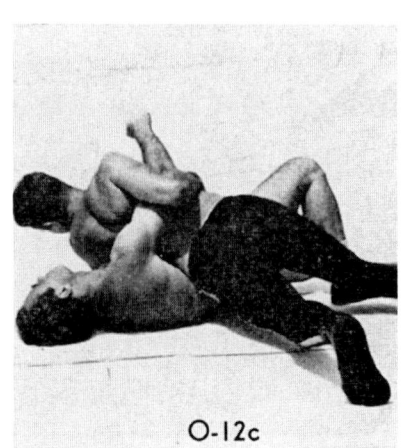

O-12a

O-12b

O-12c

O-12a—A rears backward and secures a Double Wing Lock, by hooking above B's elbows with the crooks of his arms.

O-12b—A lunges forward onto his left shoulder pulling B off balance and onto B's left side.

O-12c—A swings both of his legs across B's body and maintains this lock for a fall.

## Stand Up with Leg Lift

O-13a—A pivots on his left knee, grasps over B's left leg with his left hand, and forms a good tripod base to enable him to stand.

O-13b—A pulls B's leg toward him as he starts his stand, locks his hands, and lifts.

O-13c—A endeavors to lift B free of the mat and to drop B on his shoulders for a fall.

## Under Arm Windmill

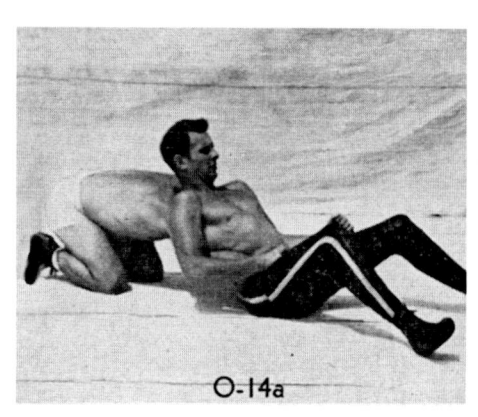

O-14a—A grasps B's right wrist, holds it tightly to his body, and sits out. A must be cautious to keep himself well under control to prevent the possibility of B pulling him back for a fall.

O-14b—A pivots on B's right shoulder, releases B's right wrist, and quickly grabs above B's left elbow with his right hand as he comes onto his knees into a neutral position.

O-14c—A swings his left arm around B's back, pulls down on B's left arm in a circular motion, and brings B onto his back for a fall.

## Over Arm Windmill

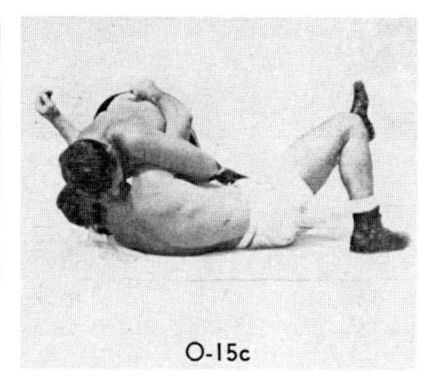

O-15a—A rears back and secures an Over Arm Hook on B's right arm.
O-15b—A grasps B's left arm above the elbow with his right hand and starts a forward drive in a circular motion.
O-15c—A maintains the arm lock which he has secured and touches B's shoulders to the mat for a fall.

## PINNING COMBINATIONS

Securing a fall is the "all important" thing in Olympic wrestling. One "Bad Mark" is imposed even upon the winner in all matches where he fails to win his match by a fall. Losing a match by either a fall or a decision counts three "Bad Marks" against the loser. Five "Bad Marks" eliminates a contestant from the tournament. There are several notable cases in Olympic competition where a contestant has won all of his matches yet failed to win the championship because an opponent whom he has defeated ends up by having fewer "Bad Marks" recorded against him.

There are many important differences in the American style of wrestling where the "two seconds" fall is used and in the Olympic style of wrestling where only a "touch" fall is required. More care must be exercised and an awareness developed against inadvertently permitting your shoulders to touch the mat. Even so, in Olympic wrestling, it is feasible to take more chances in securing a fall since you are not particularly concerned with the problem of riding your opponent. When the underneath man escapes in Partere wrestling he is immediately put back into the defensive position unless his maneuver has the immediate effect of subjecting the offensive man to a fall. For this reason there are many techniques which are practical and effective in securing a fall in the Olympic style of wrestling which we would not dare to use in our American style of wrestling where we award credit points for Escapes, Reversals, and Riding time. Instead of employing the methodical techniques of careful control and applying Pinning Combinations that are effective in keeping an opponent on his back for two seconds, it is more feasible to use tactics which are designed for the limited purpose of momentarily touching his shoulders to the mat.

The pinning holds which are suggested in the following pages are holds and techniques which are particularly well suited for the purpose of getting a "touch" fall.

*Near Leg Lift and Step Over*

O-16a—A locks his hands, with his arms encircling B's left leg and lifts upward.

O-16b—As A is lifting B he releases with his left hand and secures a reverse lock on B's right leg.

O-16c—A keeps B's rear elevated and maneuvers B into a position which will permit A to swing his right leg over B's back and touch B's back to the mat for a fall.

*Double Leg Lift and Step Over*

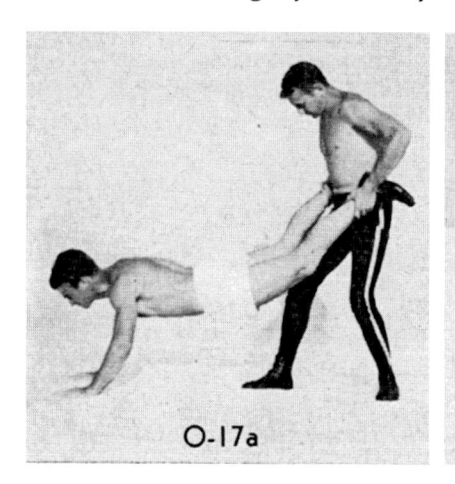

O-17a—A grasps both of B's insteps and lifts.

O-17b—A works up on B so that he has a grasp above both of B's knees.

O-17c—A maneuvers B—by pushing, pulling, and swinging—so as to enable A to swing his leg over B's back and touch B's back to the mat for a fall.

# THE OLYMPIC STYLE OF WRESTLING

*Reverse Body Lift*

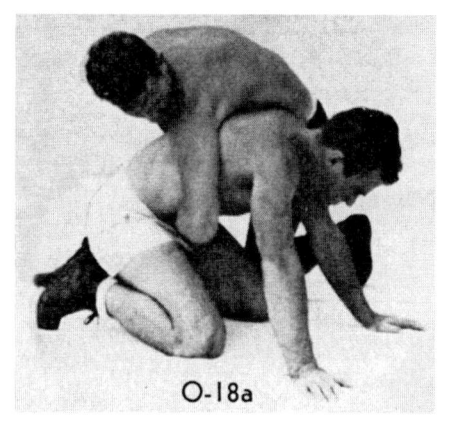

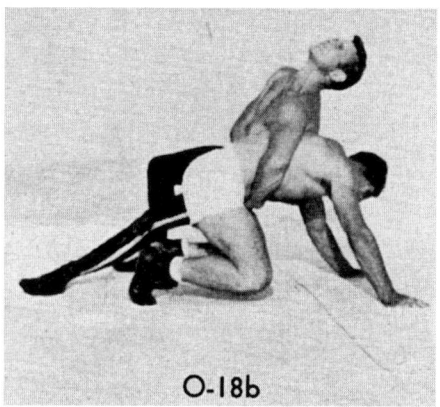

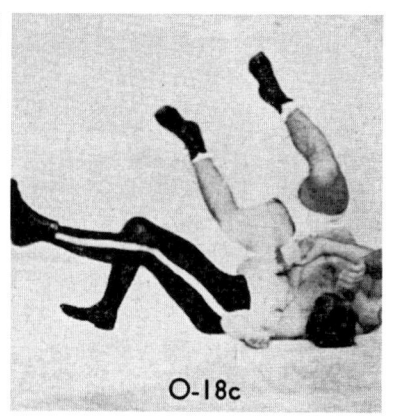

O-18a—A secures a Reverse Body Lock on B, with his hands locked in a wrestler's grip in the pit of B's stomach.

O-18b—A spreads his feet and pulls B upward and forward.

O-18c—By careful maneuvering and timing A may touch B's shoulders to the mat for a fall.

*Far Leg Lift*

O-19a—A secures a reverse lock on B's right leg and lifts.

O-19b—A maneuvers B with pushing, pulling, and swinging tactics. If A is successful in destroying B's balance he may be able to touch B's shoulders to the mat for a fall.

## Reverse Double Bar Arm

O-20a—A secures a Reverse Bar Lock on B's left arm.

O-20b—A drives forward, spins to his right, and maintains strong pressure under B's left arm.

O-20c—A locks his hands under B's right arm, thus securing a Reverse Double Bar Lock for a fall.

## Far Arm and Far Leg Cradle

O-21a—A centers his weight on his chest and applies a Cross Face. A can exert considerable pressure by locking his hands in a wrestler's grip and using B's far shoulder as a fulcrum.

O-21b—When B resists by straightening his left leg, A releases with his left hand and hooks behind the hock of B's left leg.

O-21c—A pulls up on B's leg, secures a hook grip on B's left upper arm with his right hand, and grasps his right wrist with his left hand. A maintains this lock and pulls B onto his back for a fall.

## Near Leg Cradle

O-22a—A overhooks with his left arm over B's neck. A takes a Rear Crotch hold with his right hand and drives into B.

O-22b—When B resists A's drive he may give A an opportunity to lock his hands in a Near Cradle hold.

O-22c—A maintains his lock, swings his left leg through, and tilts B onto his back for a fall.

## Modified Three-Quarters Nelson

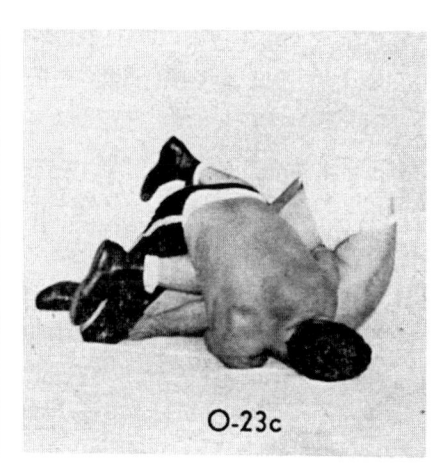

O-23a—A overhooks B's right leg with A's left leg and locks his hands, encircling B's head and right arm. A pulls B's head downward to the mat.

O-23b—A maintains a tight pressure on B's neck and shifts his right knee behind B's right leg.

O-23c—A pulls down on B's neck and forces B's shoulders to touch the mat.

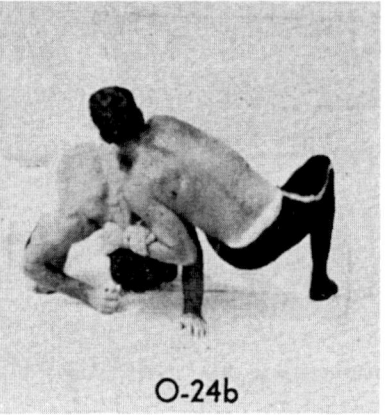

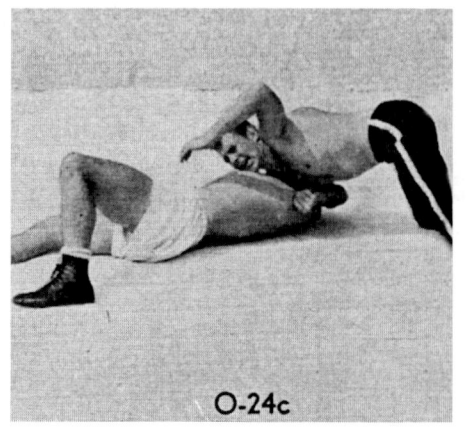

*The Quarter Nelson*

O-24a—A clamps his left hand alongside the right cheek of B's face. A hooks underneath B's left arm with his right arm and takes a hook grip on A's left wrist.

O-24b—The effectiveness in the use of this hold comes from the snap which A uses when he swings his left leg through and collapses B to the mat.

O-24c—A recovers his position, rotates toward B, and secures a Reverse Half Nelson for a fall.

## THE CROSS BODY SCISSORS

The Turks proved quite convincingly in the 1948 Olympic games that the Scissors holds can be used safely and with great effect. However, they did not use their leg in a "grapevining" fashion but kept it straight using it more as a bar to pry with.

The following series will illustrate some of the methods which can be applied in the use of a Cross Body Scissors in Olympic competition.

*Back Arm Lever*

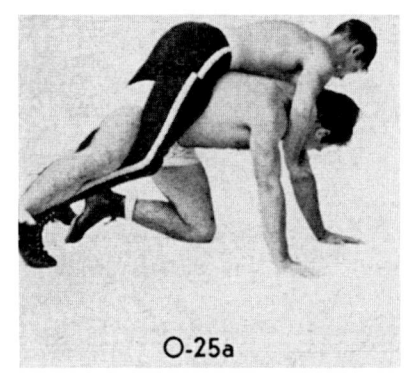

O-25a—A inserts a straight right leg inside of B's right leg. A lifts with his leg, applies a Cross Face, and forces B onto his left side.

O-25b—As B collapses to the mat, A secures a Back Arm Lever on B's right arm.

O-25c—A lifts with his right leg, drives forward with his right shoulder, and touches B's shoulders to the mat.

## THE OLYMPIC STYLE OF WRESTLING

*Cradle*

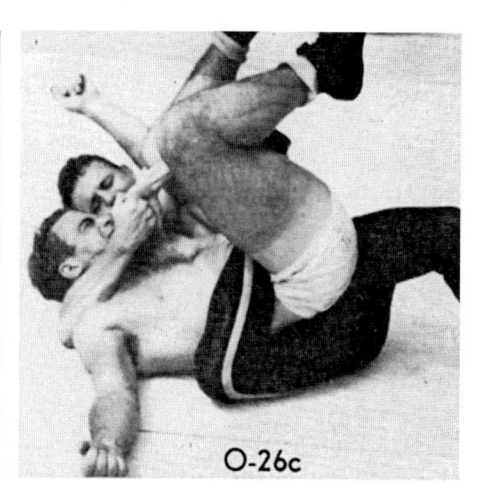

O-26a
O-26b
O-26c

O-26a—If B undertakes to stand when A has a Cross Body Ride, A is presented with an excellent opportunity to secure a Cradle lock.

O-26b—By lifting hard with a straight right leg and by keeping a tight Cradle hold, B can swing through without touching his own shoulders to the mat. (This is indeed a dangerous maneuver in Olympic wrestling, but it can be done when this proficiency has been developed.)

O-26c—A maintains his lock as he holds B in this vice for a fall.

*Far Leg Lift*

O-27a
O-27b
O-27c

O-27a—If B is too sturdy or resists A's leg lift too strenuously B uses a Far Leg Lift to bring B toward him. (A permits B to go the way B wants to go).

O-27b—A hooks securely with the crook of his right arm around B's left leg. A spreads his feet, keeps his legs straight, and lifts.

O-27c—As B is pulled forward, A is careful to prevent his own shoulders from touching the mat as he maneuvers to make B's shoulders touch.

**MEMBERS OF THE U. S. OLYMPIC WRESTLING TEAM, 1948**

First row, left to right, *Gerald Leeman*, Iowa State Teachers, 125.5 lbs.; Joseph Scarpello, University of Iowa, 174 lbs.; *Henry Wittenberg*, New York Police Sports Assn., 191 lbs.; *Leland Merrill*, New York Athletic Club, 160.5 lbs.; William Nelson, Iowa State Teachers, 160.5 lbs.

Second row, left to right, Leland Christensen, University of California, 114.5 lbs.; *William Jernigan*, Oklahoma A and M College, 144.5 lbs.; Malcolm McDonald, Navy, 125.5 lbs.; Leo Thomsen, Cornell College of Iowa, 136.5 lbs.; *Harold Moore*, Oklahoma A and M College, 136.5 lbs.; John Fletcher, Navy, 147.5 lbs.; *William Koll*, Iowa State Teachers, 147.5 lbs.

Top row, left to right, Art Griffith, Oklahoma A and M, Olympic Coach; Robert Maldegan, Michigan State College, heavyweight; *Glenn Brand*, Iowa State College, 174 lbs.; *William Hutton*, Oklahoma A and M College, heavyweight; Verne Gagne, University of Minnesota, 191 lbs.; Cliff Keen, University of Michigan, Manager of U. S. Olympic Wrestling Team.

(Note: The italicized names were the members of the team who competed in the Olympic games and the others were alternates.)

APPENDIX

# The Naval Aviation Wrestling Program

APPENDIX

# The Naval Aviation Wrestling Program

## CLASS ORGANIZATION

*Military*

The detail marches to the mat in double rank, halts and counts off by fours. The front rank takes five paces forward to give proper interval between ranks. Number 1's step out in front of Number 2's and Number 3's in front of Number 4's. Cadets stand in place. Instructor takes position on his raised platform, or if he has no platform, midway between the two ranks, and demonstrates the hold to be learned. In the first two minutes of practice, which starts with the whistle, the Number 2's and Number 4's work the hold on Number 1's and Number 3's. This should be repeated twice with each group before having the cadets kneel down in place. The instructor may go over the hold again and correct common errors of execution. The drill then should be repeated twice more. The drill on this hold should be finished by a one-minute period of hard wrestling, each man trying to pin the opponent with whom he has been working on a half resistance basis.

*Informal*

The class should be divided into two sections, called A and B. Each section could also be provided with contrasting colors (gold and blue). Each member of Section A should be assigned a partner of corresponding weight from Section B. The particular hold to be presented should first be demonstrated and explained by the instructor. The salient features of the hold should be emphasized and perhaps the situation where this particular hold would be the most applicable called to the attention of the class. Then one section should be called upon to execute the hold, *on command of the instructor,* against their respective partners. Each progressive stage of the hold should be announced by the instructor and the entire section go through the maneuver in unison and *step by step* on command of the instructor. It may be too confusing to emphasize all of the important points in execution at first. After the hold has been executed two or three times by each section, the hold should again be demonstrated by the instructor and common mistakes which are being made should be pointed out and additional considerations which are necessary to be known for proper execution brought to their attention. Again the class should be called upon to go through the drill and this time perhaps at a faster tempo. To finish up, each section should be called upon to execute the complete maneuver "on their own time," allowing perhaps ten seconds to each section for the complete operation.

## SPECIFIC EXAMPLES OF GIVING CLASS INSTRUCTION IN DRILL FORM

Following are examples of the manner in which class instruction can be given in drill form. The suggested commands for execution of one Take Down, one Escape, one Break Down and Ride and one Pinning Combination are given. Nearly every hold is capable of being broken down and presented in a similar manner.

**1.** *The Single Arm Drag*
    Commands:  1. "Section A"
                      2. "Right hand on opponent's neck."
                      3. "Left hand grasp opponent's right wrist."
                      4. "Right hand under opponent's right arm."
                      5. "Pull, drop on your right hip and grab opponent's right knee."
                      6. "Drive into opponent and flatten him down."
    Note: For a complete description of this hold see page 34.

**2.** *The Side Roll*
    Commands:  1. "Section A, underneath, in referee's position."
                      2. "Pivot on your left knee."
                      3. "Plant your right foot out in front."
                      4. "Have you got a good base?"
                      5. "With right hand grasp opponent's right wrist."
                      6. "Swing through with your right knee."
                      7. "Drive your legs out perpendicular."
                      8. "Roll toward opponent's legs."
                      9. "Take an Inside Crotch with your right hand."
                    10. "Pin him with a Cradle."
    Note: For a complete description of this hold see page 94.

**3.** *The Crotch Pry Break Down*—**Completed with a Near Bar Lock Ride**
    Commands:  1. "Section A, Riding, in referee's position."
                      2. "Place right knee behind opponent."
                      3. "Lift up on opponent's inside right thigh."
                      4. "Pull on opponent's left arm and heave him down."
                      5. "Keep on your knees; control your balance."
                      6. "Let opponent make next move."
                      7. "Grasp his left wrist and drive forward."
                      8. "Catch deeply around his waist with your right arm."
                      9. "Ride him; keep your weight distributed."
    Note: For a complete description of this hold see page 67.

### 4. The Bar Lock and Half Nelson

Commands:
1. "Section A, riding in referee's position."
2. "Take a Bar Lock Ride."
3. "Drive opponent forward; keep your balance."
4. "Pivot on your chest and shift to opponent's right side."
5. "Drive your right hand under opponent's right elbow."
6. "Plant right hand on opponent's head."
7. "Pull his head toward you."
8. "Drive right arm through for a *deep* Half Nelson."
9. "Pull up on his head; keep perpendicular; push off your toes."
10. "B, try to get out."

Note: For a complete description of this hold see page 77.

After drills have been repeated once or twice, the commands may be shortened and the announced steps reduced. Observe closely how well the hold is being executed and gauge your remarks of instruction accordingly. Caution against offering too much or too little resistance. It must be explained that the section on defense must "react" to the situation normally and simulate resistance to the extent necessary so that the offensive man will get the "feel" of the hold (passive resistance). The block or counter for any hold should not be shown until the hold has been practiced thoroughly and some degree in precision of execution acquired.

### Give Them Plenty of Work

Do not make a lecture course out of your class. The men will learn more in five minutes of actual wrestling than you can explain to them in an hour. As in most sports, practice is of much more value than the mere theoretical knowledge of how a thing should be done. It would be possible for them to learn every detail in perfect execution of a hold and still not be able to use it in competition unless they have tested it under fire several times and against different opponents. Give them plenty of work every day.

### Creating and Maintaining Interest

Wrestling can be made highly interesting in class instruction, and it must be made interesting to get good results. The instructor should have his material well prepared, be dynamic in his presentation, and show his enthusiasm. The utmost patience is required in teaching wrestling to beginners. If you have a class that is not responding, do not shout and harangue the members; besides spoiling your own disposition, you may create a dislike for the sport. However, strict discipline must be maintained and no laughing, loud talking or "horse play" should be tolerated during drills. Three or four opportunities for competition in some form or other should be provided for every class. There are numerous wrestling games that can be worked up and used which will provide practice in wrestling, competition, and fun at the same time. In addition to having such special games, competition should be held in various phases of wrestling as it is learned. Competition can be held in Take Downs, in attempting to Escape from the underneath position, escaping from the standing position when opponent is behind, etc. *Do not neglect competition; it is the greatest stimulating factor there is for arousing interest.*

## LESSON PLANS

In preparing your lesson plans for the daily class drills, it is better to have it so arranged that somewhat of a cross-section of the sport can be presented each day. Do not spend the entire period on Take Downs, Escapes, Rides, or any other one particular phase of wrestling, but rather have your lesson plan worked out so something new can be presented from two or three of these different positions each day. Experience has shown that in this way a class will get a better conception of the sport, a more comprehensive idea of the objectives in wrestling, and greater understanding of how to correlate the progressive stages into the completed maneuver.

These lesson plans are included as a guide in teaching. The facilities, local conditions or needs of the particular group may alter a strict compliance with the lesson plans herein included. However, a safe rule to follow is not to give more than the class can comprehend and be able to execute with some degree of precision. If it is impossible for a large majority of the class to learn at the rate the material is given, more time should be permitted for practice and drills. Do not make the mistake of going too fast.

The relative time to be spent in the teaching and practice of each maneuver is given on a percentage basis in what is considered its relative importance.

The following lesson plans are drawn up on a basis of having forty-five minutes' time for each period of instruction. If a shorter period of instruction is given, some of the teaching material may be eliminated. If a longer period than forty-five minutes is available, more practice can be given to the material in accordance with the time percentage.

The final lesson at each stage of training should be devoted to a tournament, dual meets between classes or sections of a class, or to some other form of organized competition.

It is most important that the cadets progress at the same rate through their several stages of training. If the various groups should not make similar preparations as they advance from one base to the next, it would lead to confusion and disorganization as they advance to subsequent bases.

Each lesson provides for competition in some form. Competition in Take Downs may be held in the nature of games requiring Take Down skills or in the limited activity of attempting to secure a position of advantage by starting the men in a neutral standing position. They should be allowed a specified time of from thirty seconds to one minute for this purpose. All wrestling should cease at the end of each of these periods at the sound of the whistle. Then the same operation repeated as many times as is desired. Likewise, competition may be conducted in Escapes from the Underneath position, in Escapes from Standing (opponent starting with a Rear Body Lock) or in Pinning. When competition is held in Pinning a longer period of one to three minutes should be allowed.

# WRESTLING

## LESSON 1

Muster

Time Allotment

Organization
    Brief discussion of rules, purpose, scope and objectives — 20%

Take Downs
    Demonstration of Stance from Open and Closed Positions
    Two methods of setting up a Leg Tackle from a Closed Stance
        a. Head Lead and Pull — Page 23 — 15%
        b. Elbow Push Up — Page 24 — 10%
    Completion of the Double Leg Tackle — Page 29 — 25%

Break Downs and Rides
    Floating — Page 123 — 15%

Escapes from Underneath
    Demonstration of Stance — Page 23
    Demonstration of the Tripod Position — Page 92
    Stand Up — Page 93 — 15%

## LESSON 2

Muster

Review
    Test Closed Stance from standing
    Drill on completion of Double Leg Tackle
    Test Stance from Referee's Position
    Drill on Tripod Position and Stand Up — 20%

Take Downs
    Setting up the Single Leg Tackle from a Football Crouch — Page 25 — 10%
    Completion of the Single Leg Tackle from the Football Crouch
        a. Completed by a Head Lift — Page 28 — 15%
        b. Completed with a Single Leg Snap — Page 26 — 10%

Break Downs and Rides
    Inside Crotch Pry — Page 67 — 20%

Escapes from Underneath
    Side Roll — Page 94 — 15%

Competition on Escapes from Underneath — 10%

LESSON PLANS

## LESSON 3

*Time Allotment*

Muster

Review
    Drill on setting up Leg Tackle from a Football Crouch
    Drill on execution of the Stand Up and the Side Roll                                           20%

Take Downs
    Head Under Arm Sneak                               Page 37       20%

Taking to Mat from Standing
    Back Heel                                            Page 60       10%
    Ankle Snap and Leg Trip                        Page 62       10%

Escapes from Underneath
    Sit Out and Turn In                              Page 95       10%
    Sit Out and Turn Out                            Page 95       10%

Competition on Take Downs                                         10%

Competition on Escapes from Underneath                   10%

## LESSON 4

Muster

Review
    Head Under Arm Sneak
    Taking to the Mat from Standing
    Drill on Escapes from the Tripod Position                          20%

Pinning Combinations
    Rear Crotch and Far Elbow
    Inside Crotch and Half Nelson                       Page 69       20%

Break Downs and Rides
    Demonstration of Stretcher
    Stretcher converted into a Front Body Scissors       Page 72       30%

Competition on Take Downs                                         15%

Competition on Escapes from Underneath                 15%

## LESSON 5

Muster

Review
    Execution, on command, of all Holds given
        in preceding lessons
    Holds performed against passive resistance                         50%

No-Fall Wrestling                                             Page 128      50%

# WRESTLING

## LESSON 6

Muster

*Time Allotment*

Review
    Inside Crotch Pry ... 10%

Pinning Combinations
    Inside Crotch Pry
    Bar Lock and Half Nelson ... Page 77 ... 15%

Break Downs and Rides
    Near Ankle
        Two on One Bar Lock ... Page 68 ... 15%
        Cross Body Ride ... Page 74 ... 20%

Pinning Combinations
    Guillotine ... Page 88 ... 20%

Competition in Riding with a Cross Body Ride ... 20%

## LESSON 7

Muster

Review
    Cross Body Ride
    Guillotine ... 15%

Pinning Combinations
    Stretcher ... Page 85 ... 20%

Take Downs
    Single Arm Drag ... Page 48 ... 25%

Competition in Take Downs ... 20%

Competition in Riding with a Stretcher or Cross Body Ride ... 20%

## LESSON 8

Muster

Escapes from Underneath
    Short Switch ... Page 97 ... 25%
    Camel Walk Switch ... Page 98 ... 25%

Break Downs and Rides
    Three Quarter Stretcher ... Page 73 ... 25%
    Floating, with particular attention to shooting
        in a leg or legs for a Body Scissors ... 25%

## LESSON 9

Muster

Review
    Single Arm Drag

LESSON PLANS 165

*Time Allotment*

Head Under Arm Sneak
Double Leg Tackle
Drill on execution of these three, on Command,
    against passive resistance            30%

Take Down Counters
  Counter for a Side Head Lock
  Backward Drop     Page 55   20%

Pinning Counters
  Counter for Half Nelson
    When on Back     Page 90   15%
  Counter for Pin Holds
    When on Stomach     Page 90   10%

Competition in Take Down Wrestling—Game     Page 125   25%

## LESSON 10

Muster

Class Tournament

## LESSON 11

Muster

Review
  All Holds learned in preceding lessons           100%

## LESSON 12

Muster
  Escapes from Underneath
  Demonstration of the Switch
    Short     Page 97
    Camel Walk     Page 98
    Leg Switch     Page 98   35%
  Drill in Switching and Re-switching     Page 117   15%

Take Downs
  Drill in Methods of Setting Up
  Completion of Single Leg Tackle           30%

Competition in Take Down Wrestling     Page 127   20%

## LESSON 13

Muster

Review
  Switches
  Setting up and completion of Single Leg Tackle       20%

Escapes from Underneath
  Grouping of Holds to Escape from Underneath:
    a. Sit Out and Turn In

|  | | *Time Allotment* |
|---|---|---|
| b. Sit Out and Turn Out | | |
| c. Switch | | |
| d. Side Roll | | 30% |
| Drill on execution of these Escapes, upon Command | | 30% |
| Competition on Escapes | | 20% |

## LESSON 14

Muster

Break Downs and Rides—Pinning Combinations
    Further instruction in use of Body Scissors:
        a. Cross Body
        b. Stretcher
        c. Front Body    Page 85
        d. Double Grapevine    Page 86    50%

Take Downs
    Drill on execution of Take Downs, upon Command.    25%

Competition on Take Downs    25%

## LESSON 15

Muster

Review
    Games:
        a. No-Fall Wrestling    50%
        b. Take Down Wrestling    50%

## LESSON 16

Muster

Review
    Take Downs
        Single Arm Drag    10%

Take Downs
    Arm Drag with Inside Back Heel    Page 50    15%
    Arm Drag with Heel Pick Up    Page 51    15%

Pinning Combinations
    Bar Lock and Farther Under Arm Hook    Page 79
        Arm Bar and Body Lock    Page 80
        Key Lock    Page 81    40%

Break Downs and Rides
    Floating    10%

Competition on Escapes    10%

# LESSON PLANS

## LESSON 17

Muster

*Time Allotment*

Take Downs
    Whizzer Series shown from Standing — Page 44
    Counters to Leg Tackles, and as — Page 36
    Escapes from Underneath Position — Page 96 — 70%

Competition in Take Downs — 15%

Competition in Escapes from Underneath — 15%

## LESSON 18

Muster

Take Downs
    Head Under Arm Series — Page 38 — 50%
    Floating — 10%

Further instruction in use of Body Scissors — Page 85 — 30%

Take Down Wrestling — 10%

## LESSON 19

Muster

Take Downs
    Further instruction in the Single Leg Tackle
    Head Under Arm and Crotch Lift — Page 35
    Head Under Arm and Back Heel — Page 35 — 70%

Competition—Three two-minute periods
    Change partners at end of each period — 30%

## LESSON 20

Muster

Class Tournament — 100%

## LESSON 21

Muster

Review
    Take Downs
    Break Downs and Rides
    Escapes and Pinning Combinations — 50%

Escapes from Underneath
    Double Wrist Lock
        a. Inside — Page 100
        b. Outside — Page 99 — 50%

## LESSON 22

Muster

*Time Allotment*

Grouping of Holds from Standing:
    Leg Tackles
    Single Arm Drag
    Head Under Arm
    Whizzer Series      50%

Take Downs
    Take Downs from Standing
    Rear Body Lock      Page 59      30%
    Floating      20%

## LESSON 23

Muster

Grouping of Holds from Underneath
    Executing Escapes from the Tripod Position by Command
    Executing Escapes from the Tripod Position at the sound
        of the whistle      50%

Floating      25%

Competition on Escapes      25%

## LESSON 24

Muster

Review
    Break Downs and Rides
    Pinning Combinations      50%

Further instruction in use of:
    Arm Drag
    Arm Drag with Inside Back Heel
    Arm Drag and Heel Pick Up      30%

Take Down Wrestling      20%

## LESSON 25

Muster

Class Tournament      100%

## LESSON 26

Muster

Review
    Body Scissors with Pinning Combinations      20%
        Pinning Combinations

|  |  | *Time Allotment* |
|---|---|---|
| Pinning Combinations | | |
|     Bar Lock and Figure Four Head Scissors | Page 78 | 20% |
|     Chicken Wing—with Pinning Combinations | | 20% |
| Take Downs | | |
|     Whizzer Series | | 20% |
| Competition in Take Downs | | 10% |
| Competition in Escapes | | 10% |

## LESSON 27

Muster

| Take Downs | | |
|---|---|---|
|     Front Head Lock | Page 40 | 20% |
| Drill on Front Head Lock as Counter for Leg Tackles | Page 32 | 20% |
| Drill on Escapes from Standing | Page 63 | 20% |
| Competition in Escapes from Standing | | 20% |
| Take Down Wrestling | | 20% |

## LESSON 28

Muster

| Review | | |
|---|---|---|
|     Cross Body Scissors—showing Escapes | | 20% |
| Drill on all variations of the Body Scissors | | 20% |
| Competition in Escaping from Body Scissors | Page 109 | 20% |
| Drill on Take Downs | | 20% |
| Competition in Take Downs | | 20% |

## LESSON 29

Muster

| General Review | 100% |
|---|---|

## LESSON 30

Muster

| Tournament | 100% |
|---|---|

## LESSON 31

Muster

| Standing | | |
|---|---|---|
|     Drill on six methods of setting up and completion of a Single Leg Tackle | | 20% |

|  |  | *Time Allotment* |
|---|---|---|
| Head and Far Heel Pick Up | Page 47 | 10% |
| Head and Near Heel Pick Up | Page 48 | 10% |

Escapes from Underneath
    Drill on Escapes, permitting underneath man to
        make his own selection, at sound of the whistle.
        Allow 20 to 30 seconds for completion of maneuver
        against passive resistance      20%

Pinning Combinations
    Three Quarter Nelson     Page 82     20%

Competition: Three two-minute rounds.
    (Two up; two under; two on top.)

## LESSON 32

Muster

Review
    Head and Far Heel Pick Up
    Head and Near Heel Pick Up
    Three Quarter Nelson      20%

Escapes from Underneath
    Elevators
        a. Drag and Elevate     Page 104
        b. Drag and Pull Around     Page 105
        c. Front Head Lock     Page 106     40%

Competition in Escapes from Underneath      20%

Competition in Take Down Wrestling      20%

## LESSON 33

Muster

Review
    Elevators      10%

Escapes from Underneath
    Elevators
        a. Front Head Lock
        b. Arm Pull with Double Grapevine     Page 107     20%

Break Downs and Rides
    Far Ankle Ride     Page 70
    Counters for Ankle Ride     Page 112     10%

Taking to Mat from Standing
    Back Heel     Page 60
    Leg Sweep     Page 60
    Forward Trip     Page 61     15%

LESSON PLANS

|  |  | *Time Allotment* |
|---|---|---|
| Escapes from Standing | | |
|     Power Sit Out | | |
|     Standing Switch | Page 65 | 15% |
| | | |
| Competition: | | |
|     Escapes from Standing | | |
|         (Start standing, opponent behind with a Rear | | |
|         Body Lock. Allow 30 seconds for an Escape.) | | 15% |
|     Take Down Wrestling | | 15% |

## LESSON 34

Muster

Review
    Drill on all Escapes from Underneath, upon
        Command and at the sound of the whistle      30%
    Drill on all Take Downs, upon Command and
        at the sound of the whistle      30%

Competition
    Games
        a. Rooster Fight
        b. Horse and Rider
        c. King of the Mats      40%

## LESSON 35

Muster

Tournament      100%

## LESSON 36

Muster

Review
    Pinning Combinations
        a. Bar Lock and Half Nelson
        b. Bar Lock and Figure Four Head Scissors
        c. Guillotine
        d. Double Grapevine      50%

Competition
    Section "A" against Section "B" (or any other division)
        attempting to secure a fall within two minutes.
        Escapes count one point; falls count three points.
        Sections reverse position at end of two minutes.
        Section having greater number of points wins contest      25%

Take Downs
    Permit cadets to practice at will on previous methods
        given on Take Downs      25%

# WRESTLING

## LESSON 37

*Time Allotment*

Muster

Review
    Escapes from Underneath
        a. Inside and Outside Double Wrist Lock
        b. Setting up and execution of all types of the Switch
        c. Setting up and execution of all variations of the Elevator     50%

Competition
    Attempting to Escape from Underneath against full resistance     10%

Modified Combat Games
    Knee Slapping     10%

Break Downs and Rides
    Floating     10%

Competition
    Take Down Wrestling     20%

## LESSON 38

Muster

Review
    Take Downs
        a. Whizzer Series
        b. Single and Double Leg Tackles
        c. Single Arm Drag
        d. Head and Heel Pick Up     40%

Escapes from Underneath
    Escapes from Special Rides
        a. Cross Body
        b. Stretcher
        c. Ankle
        d. Crab
        e. Over Leg     20%

Counters for Take Downs
    a. Leg Tackles
    b. Single Arm Drag
    c. Whizzer     20%

Competition
    Three two-minute rounds. (Two up; two under; two on top.)     20%

# LESSON PLANS

## LESSON 40

*Time Allotment*

Muster

Tournament . . . . . . . . . . . . . . . . . . . . . . . . . . . . . . . . . . . . . . . . . . . . . . . . . . . . . . . 100%

## LESSON 41

Muster

Take Downs
    Crotch Lift and Back Heel . . . . . . . . . . . . . . . . . . . . . . . . . . Page 35 . . . . 10%
    Crotch Lift and Half Nelson . . . . . . . . . . . . . . . . . . . . . . . . Page 35 . . . . 10%

Counters for Take Downs
    Counter for a Crotch Lift by using an Arm Tie Up
        and Hip Throw . . . . . . . . . . . . . . . . . . . . . . . . . . . . . . . Page 36 . . . . 20%

Take Downs
    Drill on setting up and execution of the Single Leg
        Tackle and the Double Leg Tackle . . . . . . . . . . . . . . . . . . . . . . . . . . 20%

Counters for Take Downs
    Drill on Counters for Leg Tackles
        a. Cross Face
        b. Reverse Thigh and Far Elbow
        c. Front Head Lock . . . . . . . . . . . . . . . . . . . . . . . . . . . . . . . . . . . . . . . . 20%

Competition
    Take Downs . . . . . . . . . . . . . . . . . . . . . . . . . . . . . . . . . . . . . . . . . . . . . . 10%
    Escapes from Underneath . . . . . . . . . . . . . . . . . . . . . . . . . . . . . . . . . . 10%

## LESSON 42

Muster

Break Downs and Rides
    Review and practice of the Body Scissors . . . . . . . . . . . . . . . . . . . . . 10%

Pinning Combinations
    The Leg Split . . . . . . . . . . . . . . . . . . . . . . . . . . . . . . . . . . Page 88 . . . . 20%

Escapes from Special Rides
    a. Cross Body
    b. Stretcher
    c. Ankle . . . . . . . . . . . . . . . . . . . . . . . . . . . . . . . . . . . . . . . . . . . . . . . . . . 10%

Countering Common Methods of Escape from Underneath
    a. Double Wrist Lock
    b. Switch
    c. Sit Out
    d. Stand Up . . . . . . . . . . . . . . . . . . . . . . . . . . . . . . . . . . . . . . . . . . . . . . 10%

|  |  | *Time Allotment* |
|---|---|---|
| Escapes from Underneath | | |
|     Practice on Escapes to be announced by instructor, and upon his command | | 15% |
| Take Downs | | |
|     Practice on Take Downs to be announced by instructor, and upon his command | | 15% |
| Competition | | |
|     Take Downs | | 10% |
|     Escapes from Underneath | | 10% |

## LESSON 43

Muster

|  |  |  |
|---|---|---|
| Take Downs | | |
|     Setting up and execution of Single Leg Tackle | | 10% |
|     Setting up and execution of Single Leg Tackle against full resistance | | 10% |
| Escapes from Underneath | | |
|     Permit cadets to practice at will on previous methods given for Escaping from Underneath | | 20% |
| Competition | | |
|     Escapes from Underneath | | 20% |
| Pinning Combinations | | |
|     Arm Lock and Body Press | Page 82 | 20% |
| Competition | | |
|     Take Down Wrestling | | 20% |

## LESSON 44

Muster

|  |  |
|---|---|
| Take Downs | |
|     Single Arm Drag | 15% |
| Head On Position | |
|     Practice on execution of Holds suggested in this Chapter | 25% |
| Break Downs and Rides | |
|     Setting up Pinning Combinations by use of various Break Downs | 20% |
| Escapes from Underneath | |
|     Drill on Escapes, permitting underneath man to make his own selection, at sound of whistle, against passive resistance | 20% |

LESSON PLANS 175

|  | | *Time Allotment* |
|---|---|---|

Competition
    Drill on Escapes against full resistance.
        (Allow one minute for underneath man to escape.)      20%

## LESSON 45

Muster

Tournament      100%

## LESSON 46

Muster

Review
    Pinning Combinations in Bar Lock and
        Farther Under Arm Hook Series      20%

Pinning Combinations
    Straight Head Scissors      Page 81      20%

Breakdowns and Rides
    Cross Face and Far Ankle
    Arm Scissors and Reverse Double Wrist Lock      Page 71      20%

Work at will
    Permit men to practice on their own at what they want      20%

Competition
    Class competition, one section competing against the other      20%

## LESSON 47

Muster

Drill on Take Downs
    Announce hold, and have Class execute together at sound of whistle      25%

Drill on Escapes
    Announce hold and have Class execute together at sound of whistle      25%

Drill on Breakdowns
    Announce hold and have Class execute together at sound of whistle      25%

Competition
    Three two-minute periods. (Two up; two down; and two under.)      25%

## LESSON 48

Muster

Review
    Pinning Combinations in all of Bar Lock and
        Farther Under Arm Hook Series      20%

|  |  | *Time Allotment* |
|---|---|---|
| Pinning Combinations | | |
|     Double Bar Arm Lock | Page 83 | 20% |
| Break Downs and Rides | | |
|     Sections alternate, at intervals of two minutes, | | |
|         in attempting to ride and pin with Scissors | | 20% |
| Escapes from Underneath | | |
|     Inside and Outside Double Wrist Locks | | |
|     Double Wrist Locks converted into Keylock | | 20% |
| Competition | | |
|     Take Down Wrestling | | 20% |

## LESSON 49

Muster

| | |
|---|---|
| Review | |
|     Complete | 70% |
| Competition | |
|     Take Downs | 15% |
|     Escapes from Underneath | 15% |

## LESSON 50

Muster

| | |
|---|---|
| Tournament | 100% |

# Index

# Index

## A

Abdominal Exercise, 123
Abrasions, 14, 18
All Fours, 108
Angle (also "45 degree" angle), 66, 67, 69, 100, 119
Ankle Ride, 112
Ankle Snap, 62
Antiseptics, 11, 14
Area, 10, 12, 14, 121, 128
Arm Bar, 39, 80, 102
Arm Bend Pull Down, 24
Arm jerk, 51
Arm Lever, 117, 152
Arm Locks, 22, 47, 82, 115
Arm Pull, 107
Arm Scissors, 71
Arm Tie Up and Hip Throw, 36
Attack, 16, 25, 29, 32, 56

## B

Back Heel, 27, 30, 35, 50, 52, 58, 60
Backward Drop, 55
Balance, 17, 18, 41, 50, 66, 67, 71, 90, 92, 103, 104, 114, 120, 123, 125, 127, 158, 159
Bar Arm, 42, 43, 57, 77
Bar Hammer Lock, 84
Bar Lock, 43, 60, 61, 67, 68, 73, 77, 79, 80, 81, 83, 87, 90, 114, 158, 159
Bar Nelson, 74
Base, 18, 22, 23, 25, 41, 56, 63, 64, 66, 68, 74, 77, 81, 83, 89, 91, 92, 93, 96, 100, 101, 118, 120, 158
Basic Principles, 18
Bathrobes, 11
Blocks, 15, 16, 22, 41, 43, 48, 53, 91, 92, 108, 159
Body Control, 23, 125, 127
Body Lock, 39, 60, 80, 102
Body Press, 82
Body Scissors, 72, 85, 86, 87, 100
Boils, 14
Bouts, 13, 128
Brackets, 129, 130
Break Downs, 15, 22, 66, 67, 76, 116, 158
Bridging, 18, 74, 76, 78, 80, 86, 87, 90, 95, 99, 109, 110, 111, 123
Broken Bones, 14
Bull Dog Pull, 125

## C

Calisthenics, 18, 123
Candidates, 17
Canvas Cover, 10
Canton Flannel, 10, 11
Catch-as-catch-can, 128
Cauliflower Ears, 13
Center of Gravity, 93, 120
Chain Wrestling, 17, 25, 38, 44, 72
Championship, 129, 130
Chicken Wing, 69, 84, 85
Chinning, 18
Chin Push, 24, 27
Chronic Injuries, 14
Chumpion, 129, 130
Class Drill, 157, 159, 160
Class Instruction, 121, 158, 159
Class Organization, 157
Class Tournaments, 129, 160
Cleaning Mats, 11
Cleanliness, 14
Collar and Elbow Wrestling, 125
Collodion, 13
Combat Games, 123
Combinations, 72, 92, 97, 98
Commands, 158, 159
Common Methods of Escape, 114
Competition, 16, 20, 121, 128, 158, 159
Conditioning, 13, 17, 18, 21
Conduct, 17, 121
Confidence, 16
Contagion, 14
Control, 59, 63, 66, 67, 70, 127
Coordination, 18, 50, 92
Cotton Mats, 11
Counters, 15, 22, 32, 36, 40, 42, 43, 47, 52, 53, 54, 55, 56, 89, 97, 99, 111, 116, 117, 120, 159
Covers, 11, 12
Crab Ride, 75, 111
Cradle, 33, 61, 115, 150, 151, 153, 158
Craw Fish, 102
Cross Body Block, 49, 52
Cross Body Scissors, 74, 88, 109, 112, 152
Cross Face, 32, 40, 71, 74, 76, 107, 123
Crotch Hold, 33
Crotch Lift, 35, 36, 38, 47, 143
Cuts, 14, 18

## D

Dehydration, 20
Demonstration, 18, 121, 157
Developing a Team (see Team Organization), 15
Diet, 20, 21
Discipline, 16, 159
Dislocation, 14
Doctor, 14, 20
Double Ankle Pull, 27
Double Arm Tie-Up, 76
Double Arm Lock, 89, 40, 42, 43
Double Bar Arm Lock, 83, 85
Double Bar Nelson, 86
Double Leg Pick-Up, 30
Double Leg Snap, 26
Double Leg Tackle, 23, 29, 31, 58
Double Wrist Lock, 53, 54, 99, 101, 118, 119
Down Under, 56, 57, 58
Drags (Arm) (see Single Arm Drag), 22, 48, 52, 104, 105, 123, 125
Drilling, 74, 109
Drill Form, 158
Dual Meets, 160

## E

Elbow Lock, 142
Elbow Pull Down, 24
Elbow Push Up, 24
Elevators, 43, 94, 104, 106, 111, 120
Escapes, 15, 19, 22, 59, 63, 66, 70, 89, 90, 92, 96, 99, 101, 103, 104, 109, 112, 114, 123, 144, 158, 160
Eye Screws, 11
Execution, 22, 64, 157, 159

## F

Fabricated Cup, 13
Facilities, 10, 14, 128, 160
Fake, 29, 65
Fake Arm Drag, 24, 27
Fall (see also pin holds and pinning combinations), 6, 46, 61, 66, 68, 69, 89
Far Ankle, 70, 71
Far Elbow and Rear Crotch Lift, 61
Far Side, 99
Fatigue, 19, 21
Feint, 15, 23
Figure Four Body Scissors, 75, 87, 112
Figure Four Head Scissors, 78, 79
Figure Four Leg Scissors, 88
First Aid, 14
Floating, 18, 123

Follow Up, 25, 69, 71, 96
Football Crotch, 25, 28
Forms, Tournament, 130
Forward Roll, 103
Four Point Ride, 70
Free Style, 5
Fulcrum, 101
Fundamentals, 18, 21, 123

## G

Gear, 10, 11, 14
Go Behinds (see Take Downs), 15, 17, 26, 28, 37, 40, 42, 51, 54, 56, 58, 76
Graeco-Roman, 5
Grapevine, 37, 43, 72, 74, 75, 86, 88, 100, 107, 110
Grips, 16, 38
Grommets, 11
Grouping, 92
Guillotine, 88, 89, 110

## H

Half Nelson, 31, 35, 55, 68, 69, 70, 76, 77, 78, 85, 86, 87, 91, 108, 118, 120, 159
Head Chancery, 42, 43, 57, 71
Head and Heel PickUp, 47, 48
Head Lead, 23, 26, 17
Head Lift, 29
Head Lock, 54, 55
Head Lever, 69, 82
Head on Position, 15, 56, 57
Head Pull, 102
Head Scissors, 81, 84
Head Under Arm, 37, 41, 43, 56, 58
Head Under Arm and Back Heel, 37
Heel Pick-Up, 47, 51
Helmets, 13
Hemorrhage, 13.
Hip Lock, 44, 47
Hooks, 11, 27, 28, 34, 36, 42, 52, 58, 63, 71, 74, 75, 91, 101, 105
Hop right, 125
Horse and Rider, 125
Hypodermic Needle, 13

## I

Impetigo, 14
Indian Wrestling, 125
Infection, 13, 14
Informal Organization, 157
Inside Crotch and Half Nelson, 69, 91
Inside Crotch Hold, 26, 27, 29, 30, 31, 35, 40, 52, 55, 69, 70, 76, 84, 94, 120, 158

# INDEX

Inside Crotch Pry, 67, 69, 158
Instruction Platform, 121
Instructor, 15, 121, 157

### J

Jack Knife, 47, 115

### K

Key Lock, 81, 99
King of the Mats, 127
Knee Lock, 87
Knee Slap, 127

### L

Lateral Drop, 45, 46, 97
Lecture Course, 137
Leg Pick-Up, 31, 32, 52, 56
Leg Lift, 148, 149, 153
Leg Split, 88
Leg Sweep, 60
Leg Tackle, 22, 25, 32, 42, 56
Leg Wrestle, 125
Lesson Plans, 15, 16, 121, 161
Leverage, 41, 61, 77, 86, 90, 97, 98, 100, 115, 125
Limited Activity, 14
Limp Arm, 117
Lock, 15, 17, 23, 27, 45, 67, 72, 113, 115, 118, 142, 143
Locked, 23, 31, 46
Long Arm, 65
Long Leg, 112
Look Away, 91

### M

Maneuvers, 5, 15, 16, 18, 20, 21, 25, 44, 49, 56, 60, 61, 70, 71, 76, 84, 92, 97, 101, 102, 109, 121, 123, 157, 160
Maneuverability, 22, 23
Mats, 10, 11
Mat Burns, 10, 11, 14
Mat Covers, 10, 12
Mat Drill, 123
Mat Filler, 10
Matches, 18, 19, 20, 59, 128, 129
Medical Authorities, 14, 20
Medicine Ball Wrestle, 125
Meet, 20
Military Organization, 157
Minor Injuries, 14
Moleskin, 10, 11
Move, 15, 16
Muscular Control, 18
Muscle Tone, 18

### N

Near Ankle, 68
Near Bar Lock, 158
Near Side, 99
Nervous Temperament, 16
Neutral Position, 59, 95, 103
No Fall Wrestling, 128
Normal Weight, 20

### O

Olympic Wrestling, 138
On Their Own Time, 157
Over Arm Hook Variations, 44, 63
Over Hooks, 45, 95, 116
Over Leg Ride, 113

### P

Pan-caked, 78
Pants, 11
Parallel, 46, 78, 90, 93, 100
Passive Resistance, 13, 18, 19, 101, 157
Penalize, 114, 128
Perpendicular, 45, 46, 53, 76, 78, 94, 100, 111, 116, 119, 158, 159
Physical Condition, 18, 20, 21
Pinning Combinations (see Pin Holds and Falls), 15, 61, 66, 69, 72, 74, 75, 76, 77, 79, 84, 85, 118, 147, 158, 160
Pin Holds, 15, 40, 54, 71, 78, 79, 88, 89, 147
Plastic Cup, 13
Plastic Mat Covers, 10, 11
Platform (see Instruction Platform), 157
Point of Contact Drill, 67
Point System, 66, 128
Power Craw Fish, 103, 116
Power Sit Out, 64
Practice Match, 16
Practice Period, 19
Precision, 18, 19, 20, 23
Pressure Bandage, 13
Prone, 60, 66, 69, 75, 89, 114, 123
Pull Around, 105
Pulling Leg Over Head, 106
Pull Over Line, 127
Pulled Muscles, 18
Push Ups, 18, 123
Push and Pull, 18

### R

Reaction, 123, 127, 159
Rear Body Lock, 59, 63, 160
Rear Crotch and Far Elbow, 69

Rear Crotch, 119
Re-dragging, 50, 52
Referee's Position, 67, 103, 123, 136
Referee, Suggestions to, 136
Reflex, 20
Relaxation, 22, 67
Re-Switch, 117
Reversal, 65, 97, 98, 101, 104, 107, 108, 119
Reverse Body Lift, 149
Reverse Body Lock, 71, 80, 84, 115
Reverse Cross Face, 76
Reverse Double Bar Arm Lock, 116, 150
Reverse Double Wrist Lock, 71
Reverse Half Nelson, 33, 69, 76, 85
Reverse Quarter Nelson, 33, 47, 57
Reverse Thigh and Far Elbow, 32, 36, 40, 43, 47, 57, 64, 97
Rides, 15, 17, 18, 22, 66, 67, 69, 70, 72, 75, 77, 79, 85, 109, 113
Ring Wrestle, 125
Road Work, 18
Rocking, 123
Room, 10
Rooster Fight, 125
Rope Climbing, 18
Rope Skipping, 18
Rules, 16, 17, 21, 128

## S

Safety Devices, 12
Saw-dust Pits, 10
Schedule, 15, 19
Scissoring, 52, 152
Score Sheets, 132, 135
Scoops, 75, 82, 110, 111
Selecting Holds, 17
Semi-resistance, 123
Setting Up, 15, 23, 25, 48, 52, 92, 96, 97, 101, 103
Shoes, 11
Short Arm Scissors, 58
Shoulder Shove, 125
Side Boards, 10
Side Hold Wrestling, 125
Side Roll, 65, 94, 98, 112, 119, 158
Single Arm Drag (see Arm Drag and Drag), 34, 48, 158
Single Leg Snap, 26
Single Leg Tackle, 17, 23, 25, 58
Sit Out, 70, 71, 95, 97, 101, 102, 112, 115, 117, 123
Slamming, 60
Sleep, 21
Slipping a Half Nelson, 108
Snap Back, 70
Snap Down, 33, 123
Sparring, 57, 104, 121

Sparrow Fight, 125
Special Rides, 109
Sports Program, 15, 21
Sprains, 14
Squadron Team, 15, 17, 21
Staleness, 21
Stalling, 70, 114
Stance, 18, 22, 23, 27, 28, 49, 92, 127
Stand Up, 93, 112, 114, 146
Standing Position, 18, 19, 22, 31, 42, 46, 56, 58, 59, 63, 99, 140, 160
Step Over, 100, 108, 118, 148
Sterilize, 11, 13
Stick Wrestle, 125
Strained Muscles, 13, 18
Strategy, 16
Stretcher, 72, 75, 85, 87, 108, 111
Supine Lying, 123
Supplementary Mats, 12
Supporters, 11
Sweat Suit, 11, 19
Switch, 65, 96, 97, 98, 101, 117, 118, 123

## T

Tactics, 16
Tails Out, 104
Take Downs, 15, 19, 22, 25, 59, 96, 127, 158, 160
Take Down Wrestling, 125
Teaching Techniques, 15, 16, 121
Team Competition, 15
Team Organization, 15
Three Quarter Nelson, 82, 151, 152
Three Quarter Stretcher, 73
Tie-Up, 25, 27
Tights, 11
Timing, 18, 19, 23, 25, 50, 60, 71, 92
Top Body Scissors, 72, 110
Top Side, 17, 52, 56, 57, 67, 99
Tournament, 16, 19, 129
Training, 17, 19, 21
Training Schedules, 17, 18
Triceps, 40
Trip, 50, 55, 61, 62
Tripod Position, 92, 93, 96
Trunks, 11
Try Out, 19
Twist Sticks, 125

## U

Under Arm Drag, 24
Under Arm Hook, 79, 81
Underarm Windmill, 146
Underneath, 15, 17, 19, 22, 59, 63, 66, 67, 92, 99, 114, 158

# INDEX

Unison, 157
U. S. Olympic Wrestling Team (1948), 154

## V

Vulnerable, 56, 66, 98, 100

## W

Waist Lock, 68
Wall Mats, 12
Warm-Up, 13, 18, 19, 101, 123, 128
Weighing In, 20
Weight Chart, 20
Weight Control, 20
Weight Distribution, 17, 30, 40, 50, 66, 68, 76, 77, 79, 84, 119, 120, 158
Weight Reduction, 20
Whip, 141
Whistle, 121
Whistle Drill, 19
Whizzer, 44, 47, 57, 63, 64, 96
Wing-lock, 39, 91, 100, 118, 119, 144, 145
Wrestle Royal, 127
Wrestler's Grip, 35, 37, 43, 51, 82, 83, 118

## Z

Zinc Stearate, 11